About the Author

Joris Luyendijk was born in 1971. He studied Arabic and politics at the University of Amsterdam and the University of Cairo. In 2006, he was awarded the Journalist of the Year prize by *De Journalist*, selected from the top forty most influential international journalists by the NVJ (the Dutch Association of Journalists).

For my father

PEOPLE LIKE US
Misrepresenting the Middle East

Joris Luyendijk

Translated by Michele Hutchison

Soft Skull Press
New York

First published by Uitgeverij Podium in Holland
as *Het zijn net mensen* in 2006.

Library of Congress Cataloging-in-Publication Data is available.

ISBN: 978-1-59376-256-8

Cover design by Adrian Kinloch
Typeset in 11.75/15 pt Times New Roman by the Scribe, Australia
Printed in the United States of America

Soft Skull Press
An Imprint of Counterpoint LLC
2117 Fourth Street
Suite D
Berkeley, CA 94710

www.softskull.com
www.counterpointpress.com

Distributed by Publishers Group West

10 9 8 7 6 5 4 3 2 1

Contents

Prologue: Hello, Everybody!   1

Part I
1. Journalism for Beginners   11
2. No News   29
3. Donor Darlings and a Hitler Cocktail   45
4. *Hamiha Haramiha*   63
5. All the News That's Fit to Print   79
6. September 11 and the Blank Spots in the Dictatorship 95

Part II
7. A New World   115
8. The Law of the Scissors   125
9. "They Are Killing Innocent Jews"   139
10. A Bloody Occupation   163
11. The Middleman's Dilemma   183
12. Absurd and Bizarre   193

Part III
13. New Puppets, Old Strings   209
14. "There's Money in the Flag"   221

Afterword   235
Notes   243

"And then I said: Well God, what I want to know, God right, all this hunger, misery, illness, catastrophe. Errrr, child abuse, child porn and the Holocaust. Why? And then He said: Well, because of this and that, and this and this and this and this and that. And then I said: Aha! Yes indeed. Yes-yes-yes, oh yes. Of course . . . No, now I understand. So it's not that bad then, right?"

—Hans Teeuwen, *Sweater* (Trui)

"There's a war between the ones who say there's a war and the ones who say there isn't."

—Leonard Cohen, *There's a War*

Hello, Everybody!

"One more?" The Medicins Sans Frontieres (MSF) coordinator came out of the field hut and looked down at his boots. I nodded, and realized I'd have to come up with something pretty quick—otherwise in the next hut I'd have tears streaming down my pale cheeks, and that was really not what I wanted.

It was a rainy day in September, and I was walking around the village of Wau in southern Sudan—a place that newspapers had been labeling "famine-afflicted" and "war-torn" for the last twenty years. Somewhere on the other side of the river were the rebels; on our side, MSF had set up a camp for "starving refugees." For as long as it lasted, a ceasefire was in force.

"Are you sure you want to see it?" an experienced correspondent in the capital, Khartoum, had asked. "Famine shelters can mess up your hard drive." Another advised, "Do it on autopilot. All you need to think is, *Can I use this for my article?*"

Well, what the MSF coordinator had just shown me in the first two huts was ideal for my article: Pot-bellied children I'd recognized since primary school as the victims of starvation; bones showing through their skin like the poles of a half-blown-down tent; toddlers so emaciated that their mothers had to support their heads to keep their necks from breaking. This was very useful stuff for my article.

The coordinator and I walked past a poster. "Don't Fight the Civilian Population," it said, above a picture of plundering soldiers and helpless-looking civilians. The village where the camp was located was closed down. The Islamic Purity Coffee House, the Office for the Registration of Pledges and Promises, Pope John Paul Middle School, Nazareth Greengrocers—their shutters were down, their doors were boarded up, and their verandas were full of refugees. People of all sorts had been thrown together here: Refugees, villagers, people who believed in Jesus or in Allah, in spirits, or in tree-gods.

We wove our way around puddles and rubbish to the third hut. There'd be another fifty people sitting staring into a void there, sheltering from the rain, morning their dead, waiting for their next food ration. They seemed to look right through me, as if someone had switched off the light in their eyes. So that's why despair is called dull. I wrote down "extinguished" in my notebook.

We'd arrived. In the first two huts, I'd assumed a serious expression and had made a small kind of bow to conceal my awkwardness and hold back the tears, but here I spontaneously raised my hand, forced my face into a smile, and called out, "Hello, everybody!"

And then it happened. All of a sudden their faces lit up. Girls giggled, an old man shifted in his seat, and children nudged their mothers. "Look, Mummy!" A little toddler of around two wriggled free from his sister, grabbed my knee with both mitts, and tumbled over. Mothers of emaciated infants burst out laughing and used their free hands to wave.

That was the beginning of my job as a Middle East correspondent, which began in 1998 and lasted for five years. As it came to an end, while my luggage was traveling back to the Netherlands on a cargo ship, I went on a farewell tour, visiting "contacts"—people to whom I was indebted for visas, personal introductions, and other favors. The last person on my list was an Arab ambassador. In his stately residence in The Hague, the political capital of the Netherlands, we drank tea and I showed off my Arabic for the last time. The ambassador said that it was an odd time to give up a correspondent's post, just as the Americans advanced on Baghdad. I told him that I'd wanted to stop before but had hung on for a few months because of the war. An assistant came in, whispered something in the ambassador's ear, and switched on CNN. We saw the colossal statue of Saddam Hussein being torn down in Fardoes (Paradise) Square in Baghdad. Jubilant Iraqis screamed into the camera lens and struck the icon with their shoes. "Thank you, Mister Bush!" The presenter solemnly described it as an "historic moment"—the war was over. They could put the nightmare of Saddam Hussein behind them. Baghdad was celebrating its liberation, as Western newspapers announced the next day.

Then the ambassador clicked to the Arabic broadcaster, Al-Jazeera. They were showing Fardoes Square, too, but their montage offered a different slant. In the same square, we saw American soldiers triumphantly throwing an American flag over the statue of Saddam. Then we were shown feverish discussions and the American soldiers rushing to remove the flag. Al-Jazeera went on to show the jubilant Iraqis from CNN, only they were shot from a longer range: You could see how few there were actually standing in the square, and that most of the people were watching from a safe distance.

I said goodbye to the ambassador, and over the following months I did what returning correspondents tend to do—I started work on a book about my region. But I got stuck almost immediately. Reading the papers or watching the television, I would see someone arguing that fundamentalism was all about this or that, that there'd be peace in the Middle East "if only Israel would withdraw from the occupied territories" or "if America would stop supporting the dictators." And then I would think, *Well, there are good arguments for that; then again, there are good arguments against it.* I couldn't figure it out, and that's why my book wasn't working.

Then I thought back to my second week as a correspondent. I'd just got back from Sudan and was waiting at the Ministry of Information in Cairo to have my papers stamped. It was taking a while, and I got chatting to a fellow correspondent who was also waiting. He was a real veteran, and within five minutes was telling me in a whisky-soaked voice that his best friend had died in the Iran-Iraq war. "The Commodore Hotel during the Lebanese Civil War, oh those were the days! What? You don't know the Commodore?" He was that kind of man. When I told him that I was a writer and I'd just started as a correspondent, he grinned: "If you want to write a book about the Middle East, you'd better do it in your first week. The longer you hang around here, the less you understand."

That was unkind, and probably meant that way, but back in the Netherlands I began to understand what he'd been talking about. Before going there, I'd had certain preconceptions about the Middle East, mostly derived from the media. Once I arrived, my preconceptions were slowly replaced by reality itself, which proved to be rather less coherent and understandable than the media had depicted. The first time I came up against this was in that third hut in Wau.

When I went there, I'd had in the back of my mind those images you see on the news of miserable-looking people. In the first two huts I got to see miserable-looking people; and if I hadn't blurted out "Hello, everybody!" in the third hut, I'd have probably left with the idea that these people were miserable, too. And they were miserable, of course—they were all but dying of starvation. But that wasn't the whole story. The area around Wau is just as fertile as the Netherlands, and those miserable people had been farmers who had always provided for themselves until the warring factions had chased them off their land. The people in that famine camp were mainly suffering from a serious case of bad luck.

As I looked back over my five years as a correspondent, I recalled many similar experiences. Things became even more interesting when I consulted my files and saw how Wau had been depicted in the newspaper. My article had included the surprising reaction of the apparently miserable and "extinguished" people in the third hut, as well as an interview with the doctor in the camp infirmary. He worked with the worst cases and fought daily against the statistic of "eighty deaths a day in Wau." His biggest problem, he told me, was their shrunken stomachs: "If they eat too much their intestines burst; if they eat too little, they die. Even as they literally starve to death, we have to withhold food. According to medical textbooks, these people are long dead."

That last sentence is what editors call "a great quote," and the news floor had used it as the headline. They'd illustrated the piece with an enormous photo, captioned: "In a refugee camp near Ajiep, not far from Wau in Southern Sudan, a woman gives birth. In the same field hut, a starving family member lies dying." On the right there was an emaciated man, probably trying to figure out where the curious noise of a clicking camera was coming from; in the middle, a little boy crying; and on the left, two midwives with an anxious, expectant mother.

It was a powerful image, but the editors could also have chosen a picture of the smiling people in the third hut, and taken a different quotation as the headline, such as this one from one of the other camp doctors: "The resilience of these people is unimaginable. No Westerner could have survived this, but here they wait for peace, walk hundreds of kilometers back to their villages, plant their peanuts, and pick up where they left off."

As a correspondent, I could tell different stories about the same situation. The media could only choose one, and it was often the story that confirmed a commonly held notion, like the picture of the miserable people in Wau who were already dead according to the medical textbooks, rather than an image of unimaginably resilient people dealing with a lot of bad luck.

During those five years I had plenty of experiences like this, which made the events at Fardoes Square such a fitting conclusion. American and European journalists welcomed the fall of Baghdad. They were sent images of overjoyed Iraqis toppling a statue of their dictator, which matched their expectations, and they considered their job done. Al-Jazeera viewed the fall of Baghdad as the beginning of an occupation. They sought symbolic images of their viewpoint, and found one in the image of the triumphant Americans spontaneously throwing their flag over the statue.

This was how image and reality diverged, and when I realized this I knew which story I wanted to tell. I didn't want to write a book explaining how the Arab world could become democratic, how tolerant or intolerant Islam is, or who is right or wrong in the conflict between Israel and Palestine. I wanted to write the opposite—a book that shows how difficult it is to say anything meaningful on such a major issue as the Middle East. Or, perhaps, simply a book about all those moments I found myself thinking, *Hello, everybody!*

PART I

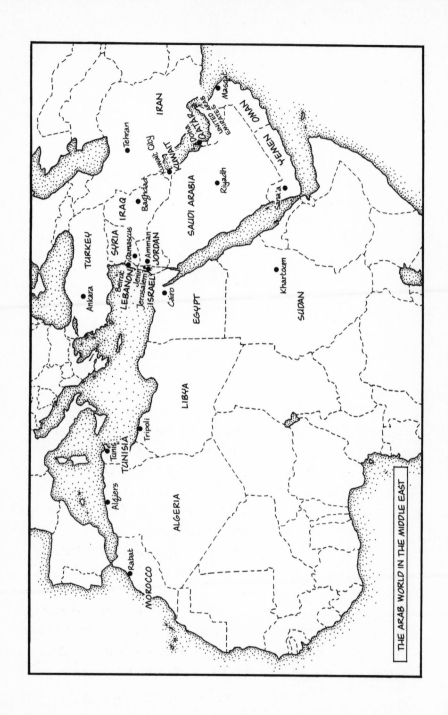

THE ARAB WORLD IN THE MIDDLE EAST

Chapter One

Journalism for Beginners

Most correspondents learn the trade in their own country, and are sent out into the world afterwards. I did it differently: I studied not journalism but social sciences and Arabic. As part of my course, I spent a year at Cairo University. After that I wrote a book about it, and that's how the *Volkskrant* newspaper and Radio 1 News came by my name.

This meant I was very inexperienced when I arrived at my posting in Cairo. Although they'd let me do a few days' work experience at the paper's and the radio's offices before I'd left for Egypt, I still regarded journalism like the average reader, viewer, or listener did. Journalists know what's going on in the world, I thought; the news gives an overview of these events, and it is possible to keep that overview objective.

Very few of these ideas survived intact in the years that followed. "Doing" Israel and Palestine destroyed my belief in the possibility of impartial news. In the years that preceded that particular posting—from my first week in Wau to the 9/11 attacks and their aftermath—I learned that good journalism is a contradiction in terms in the Arab world, and this means that you *can't* know what is happening there. You can't know as a journalist, and you really can't know as a viewer, reader, or listener.

It was something I discovered gradually, and certain things only became clear in hindsight, but my doubts had set in early on, during all the stress unleashed by waking up one day and discovering I was a Middle East correspondent.

That first week in Cairo, there I was amongst my unopened moving boxes when the phone rang. It was somebody from the paper telling me, "You have to go to Sudan!" I'd just found an apartment; now I'd have to leave immediately for a country I'd never visited before! How did that work? Did they have any diseases there I ought to know about? I felt my heart racing, and at that point I didn't know I'd be visiting a famine camp. Even more embarrassing—I didn't even know that there was a famine in Sudan.

The paper had called because some kind of "Islamic Front against Jews and Crusaders" had blown up two U.S. embassies in Africa. In response, Washington had bombarded the front's training camps in Afghanistan and a factory in Sudan. The Americans claimed that the factory had been manufacturing chemical weapons and was owned by the group leader, one Osama bin Laden—but Washington provided no evidence and, according to the regime in Khartoum, the Al-Shifa (Healing) factory had been producing medicines.

As we queued at the Sudanese embassy in Cairo, fellow

journalists explained what was happening: For years, the Khartoum government had allowed in as few Western journalists as possible, aware that they'd write about nothing but misgovernment, exploitation, and war crimes. Clearly, the regime now supposed that journalists would write stories like "America destroys only pharmaceutical plant in poverty-stricken Sudan." I had my visa within the hour.

I booked a flight, rode in the slipstream of the more experienced journalists, and stayed like most Europeans in the Acropolis—an affordable small hotel run by a Greek family who'd lived in the city for generations. Everyone ate together, the bedrooms didn't have international phone lines, and the central lobby was the only place where you could watch television. All the Americans, without exception, stayed in the five-star Hilton, which also housed the Sudanese regime's temporary press office.

I had no idea what I was supposed to do, and simply followed my peers the next morning. They were all very genial, and it soon became clear why, during the flight over the previous evening, they hadn't been worried about the whys and wherefores: Everything was ready for us. At the bombed factory, the Sudanese had assembled a collection of the remains of American rockets and other striking visual evidence of the devastation: Keyboards amongst melted medicine bottles, blackened telephones and overhead projector sheets with next autumn's objectives. The Ministry of Information directed us to the hospital where we'd find the wounded, and to the demonstrations in the city. These were small, but in close-up they looked larger, and that's how CNN showed them: "Angry crowds protest against bombing in Khartoum." Each day there was a press conference where nothing new was announced. After all, what could the regime say? "Poorest country in Africa threatens U.S. with sanctions?" Still, it was a place where you could exchange gossip and tidbits of news, and the export manager of Al-Shifa was walking around tirelessly telling his story to the streams of journalists. "The American president is simply going to have to apologize."

That's how things went, and the bombing turned out to be good for three days" news: The report ("Cruise Missiles on Sudan"); the reactions of the populace ("Clinton is lying about Al-Shifa, too"); and the analysis ("Khartoum exploits U.S. attack"). With this, the bombing was covered, the export manager could go off and look for a new job, and the media caravan rolled on to the next story.

That story was not the famine in southern Sudan, other journalists said, even though hundreds were dying there every day. But I wanted to see the misery firsthand, and my paper told me to see how far I could get. I asked around and found out that, as part of Khartoum's charm offensive, the south was temporarily open to journalists. Because the Netherlands gives a relatively large amount of development money to Sudan, the embassy was able to get me a travel permit to the war zone. MSF were keen to get some publicity for their activities, and offered me a seat in their plane. In exchange, I would mention the name of their organization in my article.

That's how it went.

The editorial staff back home called my Sudan trip a tremendous start to my career. But, as I made my way back to Cairo, I was overburdened with confusing, new impressions. I'd always considered refugees to be, well, victims. But the biggest problems that MSF was facing were thuggery and theft. Camp residents stole from the relief workers and from each other, fought vendettas, and sabotaged the food handouts unless they received preferential treatment . . . Beforehand, I'd never have imagined this happening; but when the camp coordinator told me about it, I thought, what did you expect? It was the same with the Sudanese officials and bureaucrats. I'd assumed that they wanted to put an end to the misery; but, in Africa's poorest country, things didn't work that way. Local officials knew that Western aid organizations had to deliver the goods they'd promised and that individual aid workers" careers would be on the line if food didn't reach the right people at the right time. So the officials blackmailed the aid workers—a thousand-dollar clearance fee would be demanded for the distribution of a food consignment to the south; no payment, and the food would be left to rot in the harbor.

In Cairo I slept for twenty-four hours, unpacked a few boxes, and then it was Monday morning. I sat down at my desk, lined up my "Middle East Correspondent" business cards, checked that my fax, phone, computer, and Internet were connected, and spotted a fatal flaw. What if a Western tourist was kidnapped in Yemen, a spiritual leader was blown up in Lebanon, Baghdad's regime staged angry demonstrations, or a fundamentalist group was rounded up in the south of my very own Egypt? . . . How would I know about it? You might tell me to switch on the news. But I *was* the news now.

It turned out to work like this: All the newspaper, radio, and television offices subscribe to news agencies such as Reuters, Agence France Presse (AFP), Associated Press (AP), and their more lightweight competitors. These news agencies send reporters to important events and also have tipsters on the payroll, even in the furthest corners of the world. When one of these reporters or tipsters from say, Reuters, comes across something newsworthy, he calls his line manager. The line manager consults his bosses; and if they give the green light, reporters and photographers go off on the chase. Their photos and information are sent to the local capital or to London, where they are turned into a newsflash that is forwarded as quickly as possible to thousands of editors all over the world. Twenty-four hours a day, seven days a week—press conferences, funerals, world records, shootings, election results, medical wonders, earthquakes, amazing rescue operations, unexpected snowfall, border incidents . . .

The news agencies are the eyes and ears of the world and, in the industry, their flood of information is called the "news stream" or simply "the agencies" or "the wires." It would go like this: "Hilversum studios here. The wires say that some fundamentalists have been picked up in your area. Do you know anything else about it?" In the beginning I sometimes wanted to exclaim, "How do you expect me to know anything else about it when the local media sits on news for days on end?" It was, of course, a standard question, but the implication verged on humiliating: If, in Hilversum, they had faster and better access to what was happening in my area than I did, where did that leave me?

Presenting was the primary task of every correspondent, as I discovered a month and a half later when the Middle East really dominated world news for a while. Saddam Hussein was still in power in Iraq and had expelled the UN weapons inspectors from his country. The U.S. was insisting that he let them back in, and was threatening him with bombardment.

An ultimatum was set, and journalists hurried to neighboring Jordan, where the only still-functioning Iraqi embassy was situated. I was reunited with the journalists I'd gotten to know in Sudan, but there were too many new faces for it to be an intimate reunion. The fact was, because America bombing Iraq was more newsworthy than America bombing Sudan, reporters had flown in from all over the world. The week before they'd reported on riots in Asia, and after this they'd move on to Africa. It made for some interesting scenes in the five-star hotels in Amman. You had the diplomats and Western businessmen who'd been working in Iraq and had all raced from Baghdad to Amman in their four-wheel drives, and you had the journalists who'd raced to Amman to tear off in four-wheel drives to Baghdad. Apparently there were also Iraqi secret agents in the five-star hotels, trying to keep a record of who the expats were talking to.

It was as cosy as could be with all those war correspondents, and practical problems dominated our conversations. We huddled up with contacts, spoke stealthily into our phones, tried to wheedle other people's gambits out of them after much beer, or begged the BBC for help—there was a rumor going round that they had a functionary at the Iraqi Ministry of Information on their payroll and could get visas. This was what everything revolved around, and for me, too— getting a visa. What a humiliating nightmare. You filled in a form and you went twice a day to the Iraqi embassy to listen to Consul Sadun, sitting under a large poster of Saddam Hussein, the Anointed, the Glorious, read out the names of the lucky few. We jostled Sadun like children clustering around a dubious-looking man with candy and, on the final evening before the ultimatum was levied, I saw grown men in tears by the embassy gates when they discovered they'd be reduced to peering through the fence. Perhaps it was some consolation to them that, shortly afterwards, all the stress gave Sadun a heart attack. Some news organizations sent fruit baskets.

Back in our hotel, everyone was drinking. "Arafat! Yes, Arafat. That time when Clinton came to Gaza—Oh, with that bloke with the tip-top homemade whisky—I even interviewed him—Who, Arafat?!—Yes, but I'm not telling you how I swung that one." Lost for words, I drank along with them, if only because the alcohol helped me forget that I didn't have a visa stamp in my passport either, and I'd have to "do" the war from my hotel room in Amman.

The bombings began, and a wave of suppressed relief swept over the correspondents, particularly the freelancers. Saddam could have given in at the last minute, and then there wouldn't have been any bombings. No bombings would have meant no work, after money had already been spent on coming to Amman.

The news agencies' reports over the first bomb strikes came in, and Dutch Radio 1 News began a continuous broadcast. But what was there to report? It wasn't yet possible to determine whether all of the targets had been hit. The fact that the U.S. Air Force said it was all going according to plan, and that the victims of the bombing were angry, was par for the course; I could only report that a couple of times. But what else? I couldn't even leave the hotel. Not only was it the middle of the night, but the sound quality afforded by the Jordanian telephone company was too poor to do a cross-talk with the radio mobile.

What it came down to, I'm afraid, was me asking the room service waiter in our hotel, the Amman Intercontinental, what he thought of the bomb strikes. The man must have thought it was his big chance, as he said something like, "By Allah, this will just make the anger against America even greater."

Ten minutes later, there I was on the radio show, talking first about something I'd got from an agency press release faxed to me by the studio back home, and then about something from Al-Jazeera, which you can also get in the Netherlands, and finally about what ordinary Arabs were thinking. At which I adopted my expert's voice and said, "It's difficult to judge, but you do hear people say that this is playing into the hands of the fundamentalists. At any rate, they stand to gain the most from the increasing anger against America that these bombing raids will lead to."

The White House called the bombings "Operation Desert Fox"; little by little, I realized why. News is also a kind of show business. That's why I was in Amman summarizing press releases from Hilversum on the Baghdad bombings, instead of the person receiving the wires in the Hilversum studios doing it. "From Amman" sounded better. I learned a new journalistic term: *Dateline*. That's the place the article or report is made: "Our correspondent is in the Jordanian capital of Amman. Joris, what's the atmosphere like there?" And in the paper:

"Long live our beloved king!"
From our correspondent

AMMAN—This week could be the last time that Jordanians celebrate . . .[1]

Editors-in-chief judged their correspondents and reporters by the dateline: If you had "it" and if you were "there"— that's to say, if you hadn't missed anything major from the news agencies and you were there where the news was happening. "Nice analysis, shame about the dateline." That's why those grown men had cried at the gates of the Iraqi embassy in Amman. Of course, if they'd been in Baghdad, they'd have been immediately confined to their rooms and condemned to using the same news agencies as I was in Amman (that's if the fax machines worked); but there, at least, they would have "scored."

That first night, the radio had broadcast hours and hours of coverage, with a contribution from me practically every hour ("the anger is still growing"). Afterwards, a friend asked me how I'd managed to answer all the questions during those cross-talks, every hour and without hesitation. When I told him that, like on the TV news, you knew all the questions in advance, his emailed response came packed with expletives. My friend had realized that, for decades, what he'd been watching and listening to on the news was pure theatre.

***

I'd been both surprised and flattered when the *Volkskrant* newspaper and the radio station had offered me correspondent's posts. Despite my lack of journalistic experience or knowledge of the politics of the region, I'd wanted to believe that it was a simple case of them having faith in me. But the real reason was less flattering—the basic task of being a correspondent is not that difficult. The editors in the Netherlands called when something happened, they faxed or emailed the press releases, and I'd retell them in my own words on the radio, or rework them into an article for the newspaper. This was the reason my editors found it more important that I could be reached in the place itself than that I knew what was going on. The news agencies provided enough information for you to be able to write or talk your way through any crisis or summit meeting.

It required some getting used to, and the notion I'd had of journalism, news, and the media took its first knock. I'd imagined correspondents to be historians-of-the-moment. When something important happened, they'd go after it, find out what was going on, and report on it. But I didn't go off to find out what was going on; that had been done long before. I went along to present an on-the-spot report. I never would have suspected it beforehand, but it was logical—every day there are thousands of press conferences, summits, funerals, demonstrations, attacks, and riots. How could the editorial teams have an overview of all of this? And besides, there are several thousand news teams worldwide; imagine if they all attended a press conference or a funeral . . .

A little while later, on my first flying visit to the Netherlands for a meeting with the editorial team, I understood why my bosses allowed themselves to be blindly led by the news agencies and laid such emphasis on "being there" and "having it." I'd thought of the World News department as knowledgeable men and women commanding a view of the world and, after serious consideration, deciding which things would be news. The people on the team were indeed knowledgeable, but they didn't oversee the world. They oversaw the news agencies, and the boss, or "chief" in the lingo, made a selection from what they had. Or, more correctly, he made a selection from the agencies' own selection because they had already categorized everything according to how important they found it—"breaking news," "urgent news," and "update."

Once again, I'd never have suspected this, but when I saw it I realized it couldn't work any other way. The foreign editor had no firsthand experience of the Arab world; he worked under great time pressure, had to cover the whole world, and had the editor-in-chief breathing down his neck. The latter knew even less about the Arab world and had to keep an eye on all of the departments (Home, Sport, Economy, Art . . .), as well as dealing with an expanding load of management tasks. What could the chief and editor-in-chief do but look at the news agencies and their direct competition and ask, "Why don't we have this?" That's why you often come across the same images and stories if you leaf through a few different newspapers or click the news channels. All the editors get their information and film coverage from the same sources. That's also why the people who translate and rework the press releases don't tend to call themselves journalists but "editors." They don't travel themselves, but simply pass on messages or have them reworked by correspondents.

Luckily, the correspondent's job involved more than just presenting news: Analysis and reportage were also expected. But how could I get this without having to rely on room service waiters? Other correspondents introduced me to specialist magazines and websites on the Middle East, and publications by the UN, the IMF, and various think tanks. Each Arab country had its UN diplomats, and local experts and human rights activists, who'd talk to journalists. You'd ask them about a particular issue and work their remarks into an article: "According to Ra's Mutakallim, Professor of Politics at Cairo University, 'People don't seem to realize that many Arabs are not against America but against specific American policy.'" These kinds of people were called "talking heads," and my fellow correspondents had lists of them and their phone numbers. You could also hire a fixer, a local who would arrange meetings for you and interpret if necessary, at a cost of between one hundred and two hundred dollars a day.

My peers helped me with my first analyzes, and I looked to them for my first pieces of reporting. Most useful were their lists of ready-made stories: "Have you already done a piece on . . . drug abuse in the Yemen / honour killings in Jordan / the personality cult of the Syrian president / AIDS awareness in Egypt? Call me tomorrow—I've got all the contacts."

There was also a databank called Lexis Nexis, where you could buy articles from almost every big Western newspaper from recent years. This was a goldmine of ideas and background information, and in practice it went like this: On Reuters or in the *New York Times,* I would read about a UN report on the underage orphans who were collecting the rubbish for 22 million inhabitants in Cairo. Then I'd have Lexis Nexis mail me twenty articles about the rubbish collectors, and I'd mine these for relevant facts and figures—the number of children, the illnesses and fatalities caused by poisonous fumes, the estimated costs of alternative waste-collection solutions. Next, I'd jot down the names of the UN workers and other spokesmen quoted, get their phone numbers from other journalists or the Internet, and give them a call. The times I waited a few days before doing the footwork I'd find that other correspondents were ahead of me in the same game, and by then the functionaries would have seen so many of us they could recite their perfect quotes in their sleep. Finally, for the human angle, I'd go to the rubbish dump and find a child who'd say he'd rather play outside but had to eat—a boy proud to be earning money instead of spending his days in a packed, roasting classroom being hit by his teacher and not being able to keep up because he was half illiterate.

***

Before I went to Cairo, I'd joked to friends that if the army's motto was "see the world, meet interesting people, and kill them," the correspondent's battle cry should be "see the world, meet interesting people, and write about them." But when the weeks turned to months and I came to understood what the job consisted of, that joke slipped from my repertoire. See the world . . . through an airplane or taxi window perhaps, but what I mostly saw were embassies, departure halls, hotel rooms, and offices. There was waiting, lots of waiting—until the delayed flight left, until the bus came, until my call was returned as promised, or should I call again myself? Was that impolite? Or was I naive to think they'd return a call from a journalist from a country they couldn't even locate on the map? Should I wait until the consul saw fit to see me, or had he gone home without saying anything?

My bosses back home in the Netherlands didn't seem to understand that ministries of information, travel agencies, and embassies in the Arab world were different from those in the West. If I went with my bags to collect my ticket as pre-arranged, the travel agency might have closed in the middle of the day for no apparent reason; the ticket just wouldn't be there, or it would show the wrong destination or the wrong return date. The passport photographer on the corner of my street became my best friend, or at least I became his, and soon I'd written down my passport information so many times I knew it off by heart. Sometimes I felt more like a Boy Scout than a correspondent.

And then there were the *interesting people* I was supposed to report on . . . I met people who were undeniably fascinating, such as Hassan Nasrallah, the secretary-general of Hezbollah in Lebanon. Only fifteen years previously, his kindred spirits were abducting journalists like me and cutting their throats if they felt like it. Nasrallah's precursor, together with his wife and son, had been killed by Israel, and he can expect the same fate. But, as it turned out, an interview with an interesting person didn't necessarily make for an interesting interview.

I flew to Beirut and learned from the Ministry of Information that Hezbollah had its own PR department. I could come along at once, they told me over the phone. Their headquarters were in the Haret Hreik quarter in the south of the city—"Any taxi driver will know where it is." All I had to do was to go to the end of the street, turn left under the AMERICA IS ABSOLUTE EVIL banner, take an immediate right, and there they were, occupying two simple floors above a lingerie shop—although that last bit wasn't included in the route description. I was introduced to PR officer Hussein Nabulsi, who, after having spent a few years in New York, spoke better English than I did. Which paper did I work for? Could the paper send a faxed confirmation, together with its circulation figures and a statement of its political persuasion? Would the embassy be able to confirm these things? Hezbollah demanded that the interview be done in a question-and-answer format, meaning it couldn't be an article in which several people were quoted along with Nasrallah, and this also required faxed confirmation. I called the editorial staff, begged the embassy for a reference, and called Nabulsi back to say that the Dutch didn't do that kind of thing ("But the Danes do!" they countered).

One week and a lot of hassle later, I stood in their headquarters next to a metal detector. First I was searched, and then I had to hand over my mobile telephone, wallet, watch, belt, keys, and bag. At the agreed time—quite exceptional in the Arab world—I was directed to a simply furnished room. I asked about Hezbollah's policies, and Nasrallah gave his set replies. I could just have easily have got everything from Nabulsi or from their website, but for form's sake I was taking down dictation from Nasrallah. He effortlessly deflected any critical questions, and I could forget about getting any unexpected answers. If Nasrallah was going to reveal any changes of direction, it wouldn't be to a pip-squeak from *Hulanda*.

Again, it was entirely logical, and for a while I thought about throwing in the towel—all that trouble calling and faxing, all that effort, to get to this stage play with its predictable dialogue. But interviews like this meant "scoring" on the home front; nobody there knew about the PR department, let alone the lingerie shop—they thought it was incredibly dangerous to interview an ogre like Nasrullah. And interviews like this might offer minor revelations if you read between the lines. It wasn't what was said, but the way it was said. In Sudan, I'd interviewed Hassan Turabi, the ideologist of the fundamentalist regime. I'd read some of his horrible speeches, but in person he turned out to be a giggly man with diplomas from the Paris Sorbonne on his wall, who seemed to like nothing better than pointing out a paradox or contradiction in Western politics: "That doesn't make sense, hee hee hee!"

Something like that happened with Nasrallah, too. His mentor was the Ayatollah Khomeini, who'd laid down the foundations of the Islamic revolution in Iran. Khomeini never looked Western interviewers in the face, but dictated his answers with his eyes fixed on the interpreter. Nasrallah did the same, only we didn't need an interpreter. I'd prepared my questions in Arabic and had gone through them with Nabulsi, who'd seemed to find this a fun exercise. I asked my questions directly, and Nasrallah answered without making eye contact. It worked until he noticed that my tape recorder was jamming. "Is it still working?" he asked Nabulsi. "One side is full; it will go over to the other side automatically," I said. "It's a new system." And before he'd realized it, Nasrallah had given me a nod of understanding.

That was the job, different from what I'd expected, but no less exciting. The paper or radio would call: "We've seen something on the BBC about a factory in Beirut where they're making dolls of Western leaders in order to burn them. We've got to have it!" Or I'd read something myself and think, *That's a story I'm going after*, and I'd travel to that city or country at my employer's expense. I haggled over a bazooka in a market in Yemen, attended the king's funeral in Morocco, and for the Christmas issue of the paper I trekked through the Sinai desert, following in the footsteps of the Israelites. One time in Beirut there were shootings on the Lebanon–Israel border. I would race there, collect great quotes until half past nine at night, rustle up a piece on a notepad in less than an hour, and ring it through to the Netherlands—knowing that the next morning more than two hundred thousand people would find it lying on their doormats. Or it was ten degrees in the Netherlands, but there I was in baking-hot Tehran, standing next to an election box and listening to the producer in Hilversum say, "Five seconds now," and then I could tell a few hundred thousand countrymen about Iran.

Of course, I made beginner's errors, and I still blush when

I remember the time I casually asked the *New York Times* correspondent if I could have the phone number of the man he'd written about last week. He looked me up and down, presumably to see whether I might ever be able to return the favor, mumbled that he might feel a bit uncomfortable about it, and walked off.

This was part of the job, too, but a reaction like that was the exception; most of my fellow journalists were helpful, perhaps because I was the only full-time correspondent from the Netherlands, and I wasn't fishing in anyone else's pond. There was just one list that everybody kept to themselves: The names and numbers of people with dodgy connections who could get you a visa for a dodgy country within a few hours, for a high price, if you got wind of breaking news.

Over the months, my list of talking heads and ex-pats grew: Tour guides, business people, diplomats, scholars, development workers, Jesuits, and missionaries. For background and analysis, I used CNN, the *New York Times*, Al-Jazeera, and the other big boys. From these sources I pieced together a picture, combined it with websites and magazines, and then put it to my network: Does this match your impression? Am I missing anything?

I found a better apartment in Cairo where the landlord had a human look in his eyes, not just dollar signs, and I can still remember looking around in a press conference some six months after that first trip to Sudan and happily thinking, *Yes, I've finally arrived.*

At the same time, I couldn't escape a growing feeling of unease.

Chapter Two
No News

It's normal for people to take on the colors of the organization they are working for without realizing it, and that's what happened to me. I was working so hard to fulfill the demands and expectations of my employers that I had no time to reflect on them. When my article "Islamic Front threatens U.S. with new attacks" led the front page, I glowed with pride. It was only a summary of agency press releases and local news and, thanks to the Internet, I could just have easily have written it in Amsterdam. But I'd scored the headline. And my colleagues were congratulating me! Successes like this gave me a good feeling for the first six months. After that, it became so routine that I had time to reflect on what I was doing, and where that feeling of unease was coming from.

Earlier, as a student, I'd spent quite some time in the Arab world. My first encounter had been in the mid-1990s, as an unworldly twenty-something traveling through Syria. Mass tourism didn't exist in Syria back then, and I'd been frightened. Despite the political correctness I'd grown up with, I saw Arabs as irrational men who set fire to flags or effigies, and shouted horrible things about the West. In any case, I thought they were exotic—perhaps not inferior, but certainly different.

But once in Syria, I didn't see any burning flags, I didn't hear a single anti-Western slogan, and if I began to talk about politics I saw repressed panic rather than hatred on people's faces. My confusion continued to grow because nobody had told me that Arabs, and therefore Syrians, too, can do some things better than Westerners. Syria might be thirty times poorer than the Netherlands, but I saw scarcely any vandalism, beggars, aggressive drunks, or homeless people. There was almost no petty crime; I could leave my luggage at a bus stop or archaeological site and pick it up later. People invited me to stay with them, and the pleasant, easy-going atmosphere on the streets was like nothing I'd ever experienced in the Netherlands or elsewhere in the West.

And then there were areas where the Syrians weren't the slightest bit different from Westerners. I was amazed to hear them cracking jokes. Of course, I pulled myself together immediately, but where would I ever have seen Arabs telling jokes? My image of the Arab world came from Hollywood films, history books, and the news; the Arabs featured in those were almost always terrorists, oversexed oil sheiks, chanting masses, or anonymous victims—not the kind of people who'd laugh. But everywhere I went in Syria, people discreetly tried to make me, and each other, laugh.

For instance: A Russian, an American, and a Syrian secret agent are having a rabbit-catching contest. First, the Russian runs into the woods, and eighteen minutes later he comes out with a rabbit. Then it's the American's turn; he does it in sixteen minutes. Finally, the Syrian goes off. Fifteen minutes go by, half an hour, an hour . . . Finally, the Russian and the American find the Syrian under a tree, where he's torturing a hare: "Admit it, you're a rabbit!"

A year after traveling through Syria, I did a research project at Cairo University among Egyptian students, many of whom had never spoken to a Westerner before. I had the opportunity to study them at length and, even more than in Syria, I was struck how much, despite their differences, they seemed like Westerners—and Westerners seemed like them. The most common topics of conversation amongst Egyptian students were sports, careers, and sex, not politics or the news. Egypt, too, had gossip magazines, talk shows, and a widespread obsession with celebrities and show business. And people made jokes.

As in, one evening, Osama Al-Baz, the president's advisor, walks past the most famous bridge over the Nile. On the other side of the bridge, two giant bronze lionesses are parading. Just imagine Al-Baz's surprise when one of the lionesses suddenly says to him, "Bring me a lion and I'll tell you the secret of Egypt." Al-Baz rushes to Mubarak and says, "Mr. President, hurry! I've witnessed a miracle, a talking bronze lioness!" So Mubarak accompanies Al-Baz to the bridge. "No, you moron," the lioness shouts to Al-Baz when she catches sight of the two of them. "I said a lion, not an ass."

My fellow Egyptian students were rather less exotic than I'd imagined, and at the same time certain things really were different from the Netherlands—just not in the way I'd expected. I knew that 9 million of the 22 million inhabitants of Cairo had to get by on just one euro a day, but I'd never have expected poverty to cause an increase in self-respect. But the poorest of my friends were also the proudest.

As a student in Syria and Egypt, I saw the gulf between representation and reality in the Middle East for the first time, and at the time often asked myself how it was possible that I'd been following both countries in the news for years and yet still encountered totally different places than I'd expected. Back in the Netherlands, this amazement subsided, and my first months as a correspondent were so hectic that I still didn't really think about it then either.

But then I managed to hook up with one of my old university friends, Imad. We hadn't managed it before for various reasons: One time, he hadn't shown up; another time, I'd had to leave suddenly; after that, we couldn't get hold of each other for a while because he didn't have a mobile, and that's how it went. *Issabr gamil*, the Egyptians say, patience is a virtue, and finally we got to shake each other's hands again. I felt guilty and rather recklessly said, "Come! Let's not go to a coffee house—let's go to a real restaurant on a Nile barge. I'm earning now, so it'll be my treat." We chatted, I remembered why I liked him and why I thought him an ass, and then the bill arrived. Before I'd realized it, Imad had grabbed it, opened it, and stiffened. There was no point arguing, and so there I sat as Imad, as discreetly as possible, conjured small-denomination banknotes from every one of his pockets. He made it, *Allahu akbar*, and the evening was saved. But we both knew he'd spend the next month staying in because half of his salary had gone on those glasses of fruit juice.

As I walked home, I remembered what an impression the poverty had made on me as a student in Cairo. I would never have imagined anything like it until I saw it with my own eyes and understood that you had to experience it yourself. Take a child you really care about—a son or daughter, nephew, little sister, neighbor's daughter—and try to remember an instance when that child really suffered. Take the helpless feeling you had then, and multiply it: She's in terrible pain, the illness is terminal, and she's withering away in her bed, screaming because she doesn't understand what's happening. Imagine now that there's a hospital five hundred meters away, where she could be saved—only you can't afford it.

That's poverty. When I saw it close up in Imad and others, I wracked my brains over why such a defining phenomenon doesn't get more attention in the press. How could you understand anything about the Egyptians without an idea of how incredibly vulnerable these people were? Imagine if you had no right to social security, a state pension, student loans, child benefits, fixed rent . . . And yet you still bought drinks for a loaded Westerner. As a faithful newspaper reader and news watcher, why hadn't I had a clue about poverty or the way that these people coped with it?

Imad and his sense of pride reminded me of other things that had happened during my student times, and I began to suspect the cause of my growing unease. In my work as a correspondent, I was propagating that same image of the Arab world that had wrong-footed me as a student. At any rate, after six months I hadn't written a single story on poverty, let alone on the pride felt by the poor. At the same time, my personal archive contained stories with headlines like these:

"Sanctions should clip Saddam's wings"[2]
"Saddam Hussein's trump cards"[3]
"Lockerbie poses a dilemma for Libya"[4]
"Israel accuses Egyptian media of anti-Semitism"[5]
"Israel is still Egypt's enemy number one"[6]
"Arab world at turning point"[7]

The fact was that I was only covering summit meetings, attacks, bombings, or diplomatic stratagems. "Egyptians proud despite poverty," "Lower crime rates and less alcoholism in Arabic countries," and "Arabs less afflicted by stress than Westerners" . . . these things weren't news. They were seldom-written background stories or features, and they had no impact on people's ideas of the region; but without them you couldn't understand the headlines or the news stories.

Not only did my positive experience of the Arab world remain hidden in my articles, but I was also contributing to the image of Arabs as exotic, bad, and dangerous. The ways the news worked meant that while I did write about "angry men" burning flags and chanting slogans, I didn't have the space to tell readers what was happening out of shot. On television or in photographs, it might look like there was a crowd; but on the spot you saw that there were just a few angry men who only held up their lighters when the cameras were turning, and that they all went home for tea afterwards. Meanwhile, elsewhere in the city, children were going to school, trams were making their circuits, and tomatoes were on special offer at the market.

In a descriptive piece about Damascus, I quoted the gigantic slogan on Martyrs' Square: "Dear Assad, The Syrian people support you with Blood and Soul." I had to leave out how, after writing down the slogan in my notebook, I'd sunk my teeth into a döner kebab and spent a pleasant quarter of an hour chatting with a passerby. I wrote about Hezbollah's "acts of violence," and quoted catchphrases such as "America is absolute evil," but I didn't tell readers about the people I'd met in the famous Nuriddin bathhouse in Damascus, where I'd sat panting and steaming after a hard day's work. I looked around the bathhouse, as you do, and raised a hand in greeting to a man with an enormous beard. The profusely sweating man nodded back and we introduced ourselves. He turned out to be in Hezbollah, and was responsible for the children orphaned by Israeli bombardments. I sat down and proudly told him that I'd interviewed his leader. The man nodded, barely interested, but then he said, "You're from *Hulanda*?!" His face lit up. "Aha! At last someone who can tell me why a country with so many good footballers has never been world champion!"

Most disturbing was the way I'd misrepresented women in my articles. Back home, there was plenty of interest in "the status of women," and you could get great quotes on the subject; for example, there was an Alexandrian judge who justified sanctioning a man's divorce from his voluminous wife with the words, "You can't get much pleasure from a fat woman." Or the MP who, denying that women should have the right to bigamous marriages, said, "A cock sometimes has up to forty hens, but a hen never has two cocks."

These articles went down well, but they were all giving the

impression that Egyptian women were miserable, repressed souls—which ran completely counter to my daily experiences of them. It was news when the Egyptian parliament ruled that women could no longer travel abroad without their husbands' consent, but the way in which Egyptian women behaved towards me when I was shopping in Cairo was not news. My everyday experiences only made it to my diary:

Today went to extend residence permit. You still have to go to the *Mugamma*, that spider at the center of the Egyptian bureaucratic web on Freedom Square. Comforting thought that everything is just as it was when I was a student. Dozing civil servants, piles of dusty files, overflowing cupboards, little men making tea in the corridors, soldiers leaning on their unloaded guns, queues of people waiting, everyone shouting over the top of everyone else, air-conditioning that either doesn't work at all, or goes into overdrive . . . Even once I get to the room I'm supposed to be in, it all takes a familiarly long time. A bloke with one and a half legs and a stump for a right arm hobbles over to me, sells me a coupon, and stamps it. Then more waiting, and eavesdropping on the headscarved women around me:

- What about that white one for you, Fatima? You have to get married sometime.

- Fatima's much too old for him! He won't want her!

- I can never guess how old white people are. They all look the same to me.

And then buying shirts. "Does it suit me?" I ask the girls behind the counter. "You are like movie star!" one of them giggles and they all laugh. "You have to go now, the boss is coming!" The final thing on my shopping list is the mobile phone company to pay my bill. The boy who helps me says, "We'll go into that room and then I'll speak English to you." We go into the room and he says, "Why don't you stand over here," and then asks a heavily made-up colleague in her early twenties, without a headscarf: "Zeinab! What would you like to do with this Westerner?" Zeinab gives him a withering look and says, "Kiss his hand, you ass." Colleagues giggle, the boy nods, and I say loudly and clearly, as agreed, *"Di mugamla hilwa giddan, shukran gazilan."* ["That's very flattering; thank you."] Zeinab, blushing like a tomato, shoots into the toilets.

***

I had always thought that the "news" was a compilation of the most important things in the world. But after six months as a correspondent, reality set in. News is only what is different from the everyday—the exception to the rule. With an unknown world like the Arab one, this has a distorting effect. When someone is shot on Dam Square in Amsterdam, it's news, but Dutch people know that people aren't normally shot there. They've been there themselves, or they know someone who went there and returned safely. But how much do Dutch people know about daily life in the Middle East? Before I went to Syria, I'd seen "angry demonstrations in Syria" on the news; no wonder I'd concluded that they hated us and that Syria was unsafe. If you are told only about the exceptions, you'll think they are the rule.

The question was, could anything be done about it? If you look at photographs or film footage of the Arab world—for example, the crowded streets of Cairo, Damascus, or

Alexandria—what you notice are the dancing Arabic letters everywhere. It looks exotic, until you're told that those strange letters spell out things like "Egyptian museum next exit," "Lipton's—the most delicious tea in the world," or "Two for the price of one, on special offer." And wouldn't it make a difference if we stopped talking about newspapers *Al-Hayat, Sharq Al-Awsat*, and *Al-Ahram*, and used *Life, The Middle East*, and *The Pyramids* instead? If we didn't talk about the Arab TV channels Al-Jazeera, Al-Manana, and Al-Mustaqbal, but The Island, The Lighthouse, and The Future? Would it make a difference if we talked about Devotion, God's Party, and The Basis, rather than about Hamas, Hezbollah, and Al-Qaida?

For a while, I tried to translate the names of Arab media companies in my articles, but the editors took them out— they found it confusing. They were probably right, just like when they rejected my suggestion of having a joke section on the foreign pages, as a reminder that in other parts of the world people were having a laugh, too: "The dictator's time has come, and God sends the Avenging Angel to the capital to collect him. But, as always, the Avenging Angel is immediately arrested and tortured. "Where's the dictator?" God asks angrily when the shattered Angel returns to heaven. The Avenging Angel tells him what happened, whereupon God turns as white as chalk and asks in a trembling voice, "You didn't give away my name, did you?"

Of course they couldn't do that; they couldn't just shove ha-ha hee-hee amongst photos of dying people and charismatic experienced world leaders. But they could include other things, at least in the supplements and human interest columns in the paper. From then on, I tried to write articles that indirectly punctured the image of Arabs as exotic baddies. I threw in an interview with the female presenters of the Arabic versions of *Top of the Pops*, *Big Brother*, and *The Weakest Link*—as a reminder that such programs are aired there. I wrote a piece on Chef Ramzi, the Lebanese Christian who was the biggest TV chef in the Arab world for a time. That was the point—you have celebrity chefs in the Arab world, and soaps, and shows with hidden cameras, and studios full of serious, grown-up men in suits arguing about football.

Those kinds of articles were readily taken up by the editors, but only for the background pages, which, according to surveys, are hardly given a second glance; or they were put on page four in the human interest column, which in *de Volkskrant* is tellingly called "It's a Small World."

I'd have to get into the news cycle, and I learned just how difficult that was when I tried to break down the cliché that Arabs are all the same and can be considered a single entity. I was contributing to that idea myself when I wrote about "the Arab world"—the only available term to describe those areas with inhabitants called Arabs. And then you had the Arab League, with its droning communiqués about brotherhood and unity, and the Israeli government's statements about "the sea of Arabs."

All of this added to the impression that the area between Rabat and Baghdad housed 260 million identical beings. But take the wars that Arab countries have been fighting for the last fifty years, not against Israel but each other: Morocco against Algeria, Egypt against Syria, Sudan against Saudi Arabia, Iraq against Kuwait, Syria against Jordan, Jordan against Palestine, and everyone against everyone else in

Lebanon. Or take the local stereotypes, another indication of underlying differences: Iraqis are said to be merciless but brave; Gulf Arabs, generous but hypocritical; Lebanese, cosmopolitan but unreliable; Jordanians, friendly but weak; Palestinians, persistent but untrustworthy; and Egyptians, intelligent but arrogant.

Even within Arab countries, there are enormous differences between people. You see it in the jokes they tell about each other: Syrians make jokes at the expense of the inhabitants of Homs city; in Baghdad, it's always the Dulaymi people from the Anbar province; and the people of Cairo never have enough of jokes about the inhabitants of Upper Egypt, rumored to be over-proud and backwards. Palestinians laugh about the inhabitants of Hebron, who are supposed to be stupid and old-fashioned. As in the story of a man from Hebron who goes into an electrical shop in Jerusalem. "Could you repair this television?" he asks. The shopkeeper looks at the man and says, "You must be from Hebron," at which point the man runs away. *How does he know where I come from?*, he wonders in panic. *They must think they can diddle me.* He goes to another shop, but the same thing happens; another, and it's the same story. Now there's only one shop left; otherwise, he'll have to go to Ramallah. You won't believe it, but he's hardly asked whether they can repair his television when the repairman mutters, "Are you from Hebron or something?" The man can't take it any more and tearfully asks, "How does everyone know I'm from Hebron when all I ask is if they can mend my television?" To which the repairman replies, "This is a radio, sir."

The "Arab world" is as diverse as this, but colleagues and friends back home would have no idea. How could they? They would faithfully follow the news and would often know all the political maneuvers at a recent Arab summit. But the fact that the word "Arab" refers to a language, Arabic, and not to a belief, and that there are millions of Christian Arabs, too, including the host of that summit, is something they would not know. Let alone that there were hundreds of thousands of Arab Jews who used to live all over the Middle East until the creation of Israel.

After a major earthquake in Turkey, a distinguished foreign commentator called me to ask if I wanted to go to the disaster site. "Why?" I asked in amazement. "Well, with your knowledge of Arabic . . ." Upon which I had to explain that Dutch is closer to Turkish than Arabic is. I came across the same misunderstanding later in Iran, where they speak Persian and where you make as good an impression speaking Arabic as you do speaking German in the Netherlands.

The ignorance of even loyal readers was sometimes so great that it seemed beyond remedy. But there were occasional opportunities—for example, when the next Arab League summit turned into a fight. When, as usual, the news presenter asked about the "hopeless division," there was the chance to skip the diplomatic disputes of the day, and talk about the differences between the twenty Arab countries, who weren't so much divided as holding opposing interests. It makes quite a difference if you have oil and gas or not, enough water or not, if you've been occupied by colonial powers, or you have to share rivers. Or if you have a border with Israel, Turkey, Iran, or the Straits of Gibraltar.

Planting tidbits of information like this was something, but not much. News has to be fast and concise, which is why the following article on language had to wait years in the "background" file on my computer before finding a place in the newspaper:

Arabs are sometimes seen as a single unit, but the fact is they don't even understand each other. Don't they speak the same language? Hmmm. Actually, Arabic is made up of three different languages. There's the classical Arabic of the Koran that almost nobody knows and in which you can't hold a normal conversation. That's why there's Modern Standard Arabic (MSA), a simplified form of the classical version used for reading and writing, news, speeches, subtitles, and literature. The advantage is that it's the same everywhere in the Arab world. The disadvantage is that it's actually a dead language and is just as unusable for normal conversations as classical Arabic—that is, if you know it, because there's a second disadvantage: Only half of the Arab population can read and write. Amongst themselves, Arabs speak dialects, and these are so different that you can't talk about a single language. For example, "good" is *djayid* in MSA, *kwayis* in Egyptian, *zein* in Iraqi, and *mnih* in Palestinian. "I'd like to buy some bread," is

Brit nashri khubz in Moroccan

Uridu an ahstiri khubzan in MSA

'Ayez ashtiri 'eesh in Egyptian.

Spot the seven differences, and remember that the pronunciation differs as well. For example, in Cairo they swallow the difficult "q," while in other Arab countries they pronounce it or deform it into a different sound. This might result in misunderstandings, like when the Sudanese go out into the street to celebrate *istiqlal*—independence. The Sudanese pronounce the "q" almost like a "rh," giving "hip hip hooray, we're celebrating *istirhlal*." Which for other Arabs means "exploitation."

I've probably profited from the ignorance about the Arab world. They've never said so, but I get the impression that the *Volkskrant* might have had its doubts about sending such an inexperienced guy to the Arab world. I imagine the head honcho pointing out my knowledge of Arabic, and this being what swung it. It was probably just as well that they didn't know that, outside of the Cairo city limits, I could hardly understand a word of the various dialects.

Chapter Three

Donor Darlings and a Hitler Cocktail

For a short while, I thought I'd cracked the problem of journalism in the Arab world: News only shows what deviates from the norm, and if the norm is not known, you get a distorted image.

But I continued to feel uneasy. For a while I thought it might be guilt; I'd expected to be able to pick up again the friendships from my student days, but it hadn't happened. As a student I'd been able to minimize the difference between myself and my poverty-stricken fellow students by renting a room in a working-class suburb. I'd looked down on the Western expats living on Zamalek, the elite island in the Nile, with youthful scorn. But when I became a correspondent, that's where I went to live. As a student, adopting the Arab pace of life was wonderful: Taking time for other people, turning up late, making endless calls to see how things were. But now I had editors back home, and the media are organized like a factory. Or rather, an army—it's not for nothing that we use the term *dead*line.

When we met I noticed how little I, as an educated Westerner, had in common with my old friends. And there was that unbridgeable financial gulf. The rent I paid each month was the equivalent of what some people lived on for three years. Move somewhere else then, you might say; but after a day's hard work, I yearned for the peace and comfort of Zamalek.

Finding time to make new friends just wasn't possible either. I covered ten countries, all of which required regular visits. A coup could happen at any time, a leader might die, or something might blow up, and then I'd have to work late or scurry over there—which is not very helpful when you're trying to build a friendship. In my free time, I simply didn't feel like hanging out with the people I was reporting on. How many group tirades against an American president or an Israeli prime minister could a man take? It was a *Catch 22* situation: In order to hear what was going on, I needed "local contacts"; yet I'd only get those contacts if I lived in a way that was incompatible with the life of a correspondent.

But it was more than simple guilt, and it got worse when I discovered something strange. Dutch news teams, me included, fed on the selection of news made by quality media sources like CNN, the BBC, and the *New York Times*. We did that on the assumption that their correspondents understood the Arab world and commanded a view of it—but many of them turned out not to speak Arabic, or at least not enough to be able to have a conversation in it or to follow the local media. Many of the top dogs at CNN, the BBC, the *Independent*, the *Guardian*, the *New Yorker*, and the *New York Times* were more often than not dependent on assistants and translators.

The correspondents from the quality media lived, like me, in the nicest areas of the city. So let's turn that around. Imagine that a Moroccan correspondent who speaks neither English nor any European language is sent to London. He goes to live in a posh house in Kensington, where he spends his free time and makes friends—all of whom have to speak Arabic. His children go to an Arabic school, and his wife joins the Arab Women's Circle. What kind of impression of the U.K. would such a correspondent get? He can't understand talk shows, election debates, or speeches given by the queen, or the prime minister, or the coach of the national football team. He can't understand conversations in the street, the news, current affairs columns, soaps, jokes, or comedians. He keeps up with the press through a translation service; what they don't translate, he doesn't know. He can't talk to ordinary British people—only Arab expats, British Arabs, Arab British, British people married to Arabs and, of course, fellow journalists from the Arab world. And that's in a free country, where people being interviewed don't have to worry about their interpreter's other job in the secret services.

Many Western correspondents in the Arab world seem to work and live according to the precepts of this thought experiment of a Moroccan in the U.K. I once traveled alongside a BBC hero. The local assistant took him to the airport, where he sat down to wait for his business-class flight in the business-class lounge. When he reached his destination, an assistant helped him through customs with his bags, after which his usual chauffeur drove him to the office so he could go through the cuttings from the translation service. It was an efficient way of doing things, and the BBC guy surely got to know more than I did. But how many ordinary people did he speak to and what did he see of everyday life? I spent at least an hour sweating in the passport-checking queue, and then in another queue, and then I had to get my own luggage off the conveyor belt . . .

The discovery that my peers and I were viewing "our" areas with blinkers on was painful, but it didn't explain that feeling of something not being right. I began to suspect that there wasn't just something wrong with what remained out of the frame in our coverage of the Arab world, but also with what was in the frame. Remember those lists that correspondents had of human rights activists, scholars, and other talking heads? Using their views for the news seemed like straightforward journalism—but was it?

Egypt and other Arab countries are police states where scholars are screened by the secret services before being appointed; it is an open secret that many academics have their connections, not their abilities, to thank for their jobs. Arab embassies in Western countries also keep an eye on the media, so being quoted is a risky business for academics— but it also has its attractions. An Arab academic who turns up frequently in renowned Western newspapers and magazines or on TV gets invited to multicultural arts events, think tanks, and academic institutions in the West. This means a visa, which means future visas will also be much easier to obtain. It means a free flight, tax-free shopping, and contact with publishers, sponsors, and institutions that give out work, travel, and living-cost bursaries. The daily allowances at Western conferences are often more than a month's salary for academics from Arab countries.

An academic from the Arab world is different from an academic living in the West, and the same goes for human rights activists. They do earn a good wage, because it is paid for by Western governments ("donors" in the jargon). Local human rights activists are much quoted by correspondents because, let's face it, it's nice to have your questions answered for once. But the more of these activists I met, the less enthusiastic I became—with their routine one-liners, the way they immediately handed over their business cards in order to make sure that I'd spell their names and organizations correctly. The interviews they gave frequently included expressions like, "It's a long way off, but we're working towards it," or "Giving up is simply not an option." I began to suspect that they'd read their interviews later on the Internet and thought, *Hey, those Western journalists always use that bit about "never giving up," so I'll keep saying it.*

That's the problem with human rights activists in the Arab world. Rich Arabs donate billions every year to Islamic missions and the building of mosques, but human rights activists only exist because of Western subsidies. Their chance of getting the subsidies increases as they become more famous and, of course, Western journalists can help them achieve such fame. The consequence is a dodgy tango between journalists looking for good quotes and human rights activists looking for publicity. I found it telling that, during my studies, not a single student knew any human rights activists, let alone supported them. How, I thought, would I look on a Dutch organization financed by Iran or Saudi Arabia? Equally telling seems the term that Western diplomats use for local human rights activists: "donor darlings." Embassies had funds to spend on supporting human rights, but they could only give them to organizations with a Western political agenda, transparent bookkeeping, and other guarantees against fraud. Donor darlings fulfilled these requirements, and had something to offer in exchange. Dutch MPs, for example, would regularly make lightning trips to Egypt or other Arab countries. The embassy would send the MPs off to visit a few donor darlings, who would tell a polished story in fluent English that pushed all the right buttons: Development, gender, empowerment, civil society, and good governance. Back home, the MP would be able to write a glowingly enthusiastic report of his visit: *You see, the Egyptians do want to be just like us!*

I gradually lost confidence in the talking heads, and the same happened with the local media—another source I'd expected to frequently consult. There were stations like Al-Jazeera that were said to be relatively independent; but their news was usually about international politics, their intended audience being the entire Arab world. For local news, I was reliant on the state newspapers and television, which were censored and controlled by the regime. It resulted in some ridiculous kowtowing—for example, a twenty-four-page supplement on "an angel in the form of a president," or the recurring headline: "Mubarak's contribution to peace process is praised all over the world." Egypt and some other Arab countries also had "independent" newspapers, but they were often full of nonsense: "Foreign nurses inject Libyan babies with

AIDS." These papers could be shut down at any moment, if only because the government controlled the printing presses, the distribution system, and supplies of paper and ink. It was also rumored that certain independent newspapers were instruments of the secret services, of other Arab leaders, or of prominent oil sheiks. A newspaper can be very useful when you want to harangue and attack rivals and opponents.

One of the top stories during my time in Cairo had to do with domestic terrorist attacks. If a Japanese tourist was stabbed, the Egyptian state television would simply keep quiet about it. Instead you'd get this kind of article in the state newspapers the next day:

> While the BBC concentrated on an incident between an esteemed Egyptian and a Japanese tourist, the Minister of Tourism rewarded two students for their honesty, and remarkably enough their honesty was towards a Japanese tourist. The schoolchildren Abdulrahman Sayed and Yusuf Rushdi found a wallet containing credit cards, 150,000 dollars and a passport. They gave the wallet to their teacher, who immediately contacted the security services, who in turn informed the Japanese embassy. The Japanese tourist cried tears of disbelief and relief, and offered the young Egyptian citizens a reward, but to her surprise they were resolute. They said that she was a guest of Egypt and the Egyptians. The Japanese woman left yesterday for Turkey, safe and sound. The honest young Egyptians emphasized that their behavior was normal: "Honesty is the rule; theft is a rare exception."
>
> In fact, these honest boys represent all Egyptians who know their responsibility towards their motherland and its guests. "The schoolchildren acted out of love for Egypt,"

said the Minister of Education. "It's a practical application of the norms and values that our ministry is teaching them, and an illustration of the righteousness of all Egyptians."

Correspondents would be faxed articles like this by the Ministry of Information. At the bottom of my fax about the "incident" with the stabbed Japanese tourist, a civil servant had added in bold letters: "Attention, this is real Egypt." Not long afterwards, Egypt staged a presidential "referendum," with a single candidate. The biggest Egyptian paper, *Al-Gumhuriya* or *The Republic*, offered the following commentary. It was written by the editor-in-chief, a confidant of the man who won the referendum:

> The following event happened to me personally. A friend had been trying for years to get a visa for Saudi Arabia so that he could earn enough money to get married. Finally he received the liberating message that he'd been offered a job in Riyadh. My friend jumped for joy and told everyone the good news. But on the day of his departure there was a referendum in which the Egyptian people expressed their thanks to our leader Hosni Mubarak for being prepared to lead our country for another six years. My friend saw how lucky Egypt was to have such a president. He tore up his visa, realising he belonged in Egypt.[8]

Often my editors back home would want quotes—we call them "vox pops"—from the ordinary man in the street. What did he think of the referendum? There I was, sitting down with a certain Nabil, a twenty-something whom I'd once spent a day with in Cairo. "Every revolution, every disaster, economic crisis and war, pornography . . . You'll always discover that there are Jews behind it. The problem is that Jews only consider themselves to be human. Once, Prophet Mohammed, Peace Be His Name, took a group of Jews captive after a battle. But do you know what's written in the Jewish holy book? Never take prisoners of war. That's what Jews are like, it's in their culture." He stuck one finger in the air. "But please note, I don't hate the Jewish. I've got a good friend in America who's a Jew." He told me about his studies and holidays in America, and how he was teaching his children English. We ordered Cokes, and he explained that the Holocaust could never have happened because "the ovens were too small." Did I know that Hitler had been subsidized by the Jews? Did I know how much interest they'd asked? "Thirty-eight percent. Because it all comes down to money in the end with the Jews."

What was I supposed to do with a story like this? Was he mad, or did half of the population think like this?

In a juice bar in the center of Baghdad, I push fifteen hundred lira across the counter and say, "A Hitler cocktail, please." The cashier calls out to a young man with mixers, nets of fruit, and bottles of milk: "Ahmed! One Hitler cocktail, please, for this gentleman." The menu also features Haïti, Mandela, and Noriega cocktails. A Hitler contains pineapple, strawberries, orange juice, cream, and honey.

"That's an unusual name," I say. "In Europe, your shop would probably be shut down." The cashier nods.

"The Jews, eh? We do it to attract attention. We also call dates Monica Lewinskys."

"But Hitler murdered millions of people."

The cashier nods helpfully. "He put the Jews in the oven, didn't he?" In Arabic, the word Holocaust, *mahraqa*, means fire or burning.

"Six million of them. And he murdered millions of other people, too. Is there a Sharon cocktail, too?"

The cashier can't help laughing. "We'd lose our clientele. Sharon bombed Beirut, Sabra, and Shatila . . . We've got a lot of Palestinians living here."

"Yes. And Hitler considered Arabs to be subhuman, just like the Jews. The only reason he didn't put you in the oven was that there weren't any Arabs in Europe."

The cashier slides a full glass over the counter and says rather grimly: "Israel murdered millions of Arabs though."

The account of this incident remained a draft on my computer. I definitely would have scored with it, because Dutch readers would have gotten the shock of their lives. But how representative was this fruit-juice guy? How should I contextualize a conversation like this? In Western countries, correspondents use conversations with ordinary people to illustrate trends. First come a couple of great quotes from John on the corner and then, "John is not the only New Yorker to feel this way. At least 60 percent think . . ." But I couldn't get hold of any reliable opinion polls, and all relevant statistics were kept secret. So there I was, left with the comments of literally one man or woman on the street.

You might suggest that I should have looked for sources I could trust. I did try, but whenever I attempted to write a story without using news agencies, the main Anglo-Saxon media, or talking heads, it fell apart. One such attempt was a success story about a Dutch development project in Fayum, an oasis that was two hours' drive to the south of Cairo. The weekend supplement was putting together a themed issue on development aid, and as part of it they wanted an account of one failed project and one successful one. "I can do that," I said, and via the embassy I got in touch with a Dutch hydro-engineer. I'll call him Roland. He was a nice guy about my age, who immediately invited me to meet up with him.

Oases always made me think of three trees, a hut, and a goat, but Fayum was a stretch of green the size of Luxembourg, with 3 million inhabitants. Things were going wrong in Fayum; the population was exploding while the irrigation system was just getting worse. "They've got enough water, but they're not using it correctly," Roland told me in his office at the Ministry of Irrigation. Just like in the ministries in Cairo, the civil servants were either napping, staring into space, or pottering around and making relaxed phone calls. Roland's room was the only one with air-conditioning and a computer that worked. We drove out into the countryside in his four-wheel drive. He pointed at the rubbish: "People didn't used to have plastic bags. They still behave as though rubbish were going to decompose. Artificial fertilizers and pesticides are great, but you have to teach people how to use them. Here you've got one ministry engineer per five hundred farmers, and the engineers are pricks who look down on the farmers." Peasants or farmers? These are small and simple people.

"This is what's going wrong." Roland pointed to a blocked irrigation canal. "Farmers dump their rubbish and pesticides. There are increasing numbers of bloody conflicts over stolen water, and the civil servants are too lazy or corrupt to intervene." He outlined the solution: If the farmers were to set up water boards, as the Dutch had done centuries before in their polders, these water boards could help farmers do their own irrigation, maintain their canals, raise awareness, and resolve conflicts.

Roland's people had run a trial of this idea, and it had been a success. Roland got out of the car, walked over to two farmers, and proudly asked one of them what happened now if a Fayumi was caught stealing water. "We smash his face in!" they said. The farmers did what all Egyptians do after a joke—they shook hands. "But afterwards we call an emergency meeting of the board," the older farmer said. "On behalf of the Egyptian people, I'd like to thank the Dutch for their help," he said, now with disarming solemnity. "There are fewer stabbings now, and I have much more harvest."

We said goodbye, and I showered Roland in compliments. I had my success story—who said that development aid was a waste of time? Roland smiled. But, a few weeks after my rather celebratory article was published, one of his colleagues, well-oiled at the time, told me the real story. The idea behind development aid is to render Western specialists unnecessary, as quickly as possible. People have to do it themselves. So the Dutch water managers had pushed on to the next step: Give the water boards rights, hold elections for the board, give the board an advisory council, and raise contributions for the employees. But these would be directors chosen and paid for by the farmers themselves, wouldn't they? That wasn't the intention, the ministries of construction and irrigation in Cairo let it be known; power should stay with them. The water boards were condemned to fail.

So I wrote some things that later turned out not to be true, and the opposite occurred, too. On one occasion, a Dutch diplomat put me in contact with a Syrian MP, Riad Sef. His brother and son had been murdered by the regime, she said, and his sports shoe factory had been destroyed. "If you want patriotism, go to Riad Sef," she added. "He could easily seek political asylum with us, but he's staying here. And he dares to test the limits."

When I called him, I could go round at once, whereupon Sef shook my hand and burst out with, "Everything, everything, everything but everything here is lies. And these lies persist because the government controls everything—your daily bread, your career, your idea of the world. Did you know that you weren't allowed to own a fax machine here until recently, or satellite dishes, or foreign currency?" Sef lit up another cigarette, and explained that he was one of the few MPs who hadn't got his seat through a fixed election run by the regime. "Perhaps they thought I'd back down, and it was hard to get around me. I stood for election in the Damascus district, a lot of people know me, and no one would have believed it if I hadn't won a seat. What's more, if there's Western criticism, the regime can always point at me and say, look, we do have opposition."

I stopped and shook my writing hand, which had gone numb; I could hardly keep up with Sef. "Votes in parliament are fixed in advance," Sef explained. "Just like the agenda and the speeches. A typical address begins with something like, 'This law is fantastic—a gift to the people from the president.'" He lit another cigarette. "I'm not exaggerating. Recently, a speaker read out his notes in the wrong order. He only noticed halfway through. The parliament here is an applause machine, and the seats are gifts for loyal servicemen." Could he broach this abuse of power in the press? Sef sniffed, "Journalists know exactly what they can and can't write about. I mean, they are appointed by the regime.

Once in a while the press can write freely about corruption, but only at the expense of people who have fallen out of favor of the regime."

But what if Sef could convince his colleagues in parliament to do their work—that's to say, monitor the government? Would that be possible? "Forget it. All important data are kept secret. The military, the regime's leaders, and the president's family are untouchable. MPs get no expenses and no research funds. You don't get a secretary, or an office, or Internet, or newspapers. That kind of support would cost fifteen hundred dollars a month, but you only earn two hundred fifty. I've got money of my own; that's how I can do this." I asked if he could say anything about the business interests of the president's family, the defense budget, or the expenditure of oil profits. For the first time, he fell silent; Sef shook his head, no, and indicated with his hands, *Don't forget, we're being listened to.* There I was, a journalist from a rich country like the Netherlands, sitting opposite a man who could have been my father and yet didn't dare to answer me. I asked whether I could write what he'd just recounted, and he nodded theatrically, *Yes.*

I'd just started copying it out when I bumped into a couple of Syrian human rights activists at a diplomat's party. "Riad Sef?" one of them asked in derision. "Don't tell me you fell for that one. That man is so much part of the secret services, how do you think he gets away with saying things like that?" Rather disconcerted, I shut up and decided to use only a part of Sef's speech in a running story, in amongst other talking heads. A year later, I was back in Syria and filed this article:

"We'd like to have a coffee with you," said the two men in civilian attire after they'd rung the doorbell.

"Step inside," answered the MP, who'd just made

revelations about corrupt members of the president's family.

"The Minister of Home Affairs would also like to have a coffee with you," the two men said as they drained their cups.

"Of course," said the MP, who was suffering from high blood pressure.

"Bring your medicine with you," the men said.

This was how Riad Sef was picked up three months ago. No flashing lights, no masked men, drawn weapons, or Hollywood scenes, but the consequences were no less dramatic, as Sef's wife recounted in a Damascus restaurant. Sef can expect a sentence of between five years and life. Syrian restaurants mostly have a family section where women, couples, and families can avoid being troubled by single men. The secret services only hire men, so Reem is happy to sit in the family section; they can't come and sit down next to her here.

"You never get used to it," Reem says. Nowadays, if they make phone calls, there's a man in Syria somewhere, taking down notes. "I never have any personal conversations anymore." Almost all of her friends have broken off contact, out of fear. "I hoped they'd visit me at the end of Ramadan, like every year," she says dejectedly. "Unfortunately . . ." She only sees her neighbors now. She doesn't know if her house is bugged. "I whisper a lot." Recently, she was supposed to go on a silent march through Damascus along with the wives of other arrested dissidents, but the secret services intervened. How had they found out about it? Maybe one of the wives had gossiped. Maybe one of them was working as an informer so that her husband wouldn't be tortured so much. You never knew in Syria.

It does make some difference that her husband is a former MP, Reem admits. The others are held in an underground bunker and allowed visitors only once every three weeks. Reem can visit every week, along with her four-year-old daughter. There's a guard permanently present, and her daughter told Sef recently that she was going to buy a gun. She pointed at the guard, giggling, "I'll shoot him so that we can take you home again."[9]

The fact that Sef was going to prison for years suggested that the donor darling at the diplomat's party might have got it wrong, but you could never know for sure. A Syrian journalist once told me that members of the regime in Damascus earned a lot of money selling military search warrants which, according to him, Syrians could use to get refugee status in Europe. From time to time, a refugee was sent back because the European immigration services had decided that Syria was no longer a dangerous country. This was bad for business, so the refugee would be killed on his return, and Syria would qualify as dangerous once again.

It was a horrible story, but was it true? I asked around amongst colleagues, diplomats, and others and they said, "That Syrian journalist? He's so in the secret services— everyone knows that, don't they?" A while later, the journalist was suddenly imprisoned, causing everyone to wonder whether they'd locked him up to enhance his credibility, whether he'd gone too far, or whether in fact he wasn't in the secret services.

In Beirut, an Iraqi doctor, who'd fled his country, claimed that Saddam's regime confiscated stillborn babies in the hospitals and froze them so that they could produce them as "victims of the sanctions" when reporters or left-wing European

MPs came to visit. This was another horrible story, but how could I check whether the doctor was telling the truth?

It was a struggle; even when thought I had my facts straight, something would happen and I'd think, *No, there's something fundamentally wrong here.* One example was the Saad Eddin Ibrahim affair. He was the most important donor darling in Egypt, and had been running mediagenic campaigns for years on the emergency situation, discrimination against Christians, the regime's abuse of power, and other sensitive matters. A year before the election—or what passed for one—Ibrahim had received money from the E.U. to make a film to explain how elections worked. He'd had a ballot scene in it, and now the country was up in arms. His name had been taboo in the Egyptian media for years, but now both the state press and the so-called independent press were beside themselves: Ibrahim had committed "election fraud" and had used foreign money to "soil Egypt's reputation." For weeks on end, the press dished the dirt on Ibrahim's Ibn Khaldoun Center: "Star of David found at Ibn Khaldoun," "Ibrahim wants to make Muslims eat horsemeat." Only the tiny independent English-language *Cairo Times* reported how much proof there was of election fraud (none) and analyzed the regime's motives: Ibrahim was famous and had an American passport. Eliminating him was a clear signal to any Egyptians who were considering expressing their opinions on CNN.

The *Cairo Times*" interpretation seemed the most convincing to me, so that one made the paper. Matter closed, you would think, and the afternoon after sending the article I took time off to attend the graduation projects of the film students at the expensive American University in Cairo.

I sat next to a man in his early twenties from the Haram slum district, "Hazem." He was wearing his only presentable suit because this was his big chance. One of the students had an uncle who was high up in the Ministry of Information, and Hazem had arranged to ask the uncle a question. He would work the answer into a flattering article for a newspaper and then he'd go back to the uncle and ask him for a job. Unfortunately, there was no sign of the uncle, and Hazem had to bite his tongue in frustration. We chatted a while and I got onto the subject of Saad Eddin Ibrahim. Hazem nodded in relief, "Unbelievable, isn't it? You see how our regime has to be on its toes all the time? You don't want to know how many enemies Egypt has—the last thing I heard was that Israeli girls had spread AIDS in the Sinaï desert." I looked at Hazem and thought, *Should I write only about what is happening in Egypt, or also about what people* think *is happening here?* But, again, how could I—without access to reliable opinion polls—find out what the average Egyptian thought?

Chapter Four

Hamiha Haramiha

In retrospect, I wonder why it took me so long to realize that the concept of good journalism in the Arab world is a contradiction in terms. I missed it for years because, one, I had no idea how journalism worked; two, no one in the business talks about it; and three, which was the main reason, for a long time the word "dictatorship" meant something abstract to me.

Of course, I'd *read* about dictatorships. As a young student I'd come across sentences such as "Arab dictators hold on to power through a mixture of intimidation, co-option, and deception," or "Within a dictatorship, lawlessness is such that society becomes chronically corrupt and structurally opaque, and public opinion ends up fundamentally out of joint."

It hadn't sunk in, not really, and that was the case for a long time. During the year I spent at Cairo University, I learned that people were sent to prison without trial; I saw the portraits of the president; and there was an armored tank with a machine gun in front of the campus. You get used to such things. I knew that, as a Westerner, the regime wouldn't touch me—it would be bad publicity for investors and would deter tourists—so it never became more than an interesting question for me: Might my student friends, people I saw three times a week or more, be working as informants for one of the secret services? When I returned to Egypt as a correspondent, I knew that the worst the regime might do was to deport me—something that hadn't happened there for years. I had a nice life, and so the true face of the system in which I was living and working remained hidden. The presidential portraits, tanks, and fixed elections notwithstanding, Arab and Western society seemed pretty much the same.

But less than a year later, I became much less certain of this.

For want of anything better, I still approached talking heads for their opinions about the news of the day: A conflict between Iraq and the U.S. ("More combative signs from Baghdad"); a setback or breakthrough in the peace process ("Israel's neighbors cautiously optimistic"); the latest speech by the American president or secretary of state ("Looks like it was written in Jerusalem").

Arabs enjoy conversation, and so after an interview, I'd chat away with a closed notebook. That's when I heard things that made me think, *Hello, everybody*! A Syrian professor told me that he'd stopped discussing politics with his wife over the dinner table, and no longer switched off the television in irritation when the president came on. His son had reached the age where he repeated things—for example, in the school playground, where the children of secret agents were walking around. A Lebanese lawyer admitted that he only took on rich clients because, if you couldn't pay off the judge, litigation was pointless. A businessman said that he'd been stopped by a policeman the day before; the street had been closed off because the president was going that way. "Before I could turn my car around," the businessman said, "my four-year-old daughter had offered the policeman a thousand-lira note. She's so used to getting everything with bribes."

It's a journalistic no-no to interview taxi drivers because of the fear that they only say what the customer wants to hear. But in many Arab countries, drivers have day jobs as civil servants, so the taxi provides a safe place in which to have conversations with ordinary people. Some drivers were cagey, others more open: One said that policemen could "buy" busy crossroads for a hefty sum in order to issue fines, which went into their own pockets. A large share of the profits would go to a boss who'd subtract a sum, and so on, making a pyramid of parasites. Some drivers worked for customs, in taxation, in education, or in prisons, and the same pyramids seemed to exist everywhere. "I can't help it," drivers would say. "My salary is too small to live on."

My usual driver in Jordan told me that his brother had gone to Damascus in a brand-new Mercedes to spend a weekend with his family. The next morning, the car was gone. He reported the theft to the police, made the rest of his visits by taxi, but on the last day he saw his Mercedes with a new HUKUMA [government] number plate. The police station tracked the number plate, and an hour later a general turned up. "Was that your car?" he asked brusquely. "We found arms and drugs in it, enough to lock you up forever." The brother nodded, excused himself, and left.

During a trip back to the Netherlands, a taxi driver who was originally from Egypt told me that a friendly-looking guy in a coffee house had accosted him during his last trip home: Wasn't he bothered by the mess the country was in? Wasn't it scandalous, all this waste and repression? Did the taxi driver live in Europe? That was a rich and civilized place—our idiot of a president could learn something there. The taxi driver was indeed bothered, terribly bothered, by the state of his homeland. He agreed, and aired a few further complaints, and then the friendly-looking man said, "Listen, you bastard, I'm with the secret police. I'll let you off this time, but you'd better watch out. I know where to find you and your family."

Or take the story of "Walid." I met him after the pope's visit to Syria. This had produced a predictable article about the Holy Father's travel itinerary, embellished with great quotes from the president and the most senior bishop in Syria on religious tolerance and world peace. I padded it out with human interest quotes from ordinary Syrian Christians, and we were ready to go. The piece made the front page, and colleagues back home sent their congratulations.

Thanks, but it seemed I was learning much more about Syria from Walid. He'd been recommended to me by a tour leader I'd befriended. At first, he hadn't wanted to talk because he'd had bad experiences with Western journalists. Walid was in his twenties, had a modern haircut and good clothes, and his father had lived in England for a while. We had a beer together in the hotel bar, and strolled on to a night-club. What was it like to be a pro-Western young man living in Syria? He looked at me as if I was asking him whether Syria would ever win the World Cup. "It's really boring. Boring, boring, boring. Every day you see the same slogans; you hear the same incendiary rubbish about Israel, while everyone knows that we'll never be able to do anything for the Palestinians. Everybody's cynical. They're selling degrees for three hundred dollars a subject at the university. Professors force students to have sex with them in exchange for good grades. Sons of important fathers pass all their subjects without taking the exams. You've worked damn hard and he hasn't. You get a nice grade but he gets a great grade, because his dad's put in a call to the professor. Wouldn't that drive you mad?"

What did he feel when he saw a portrait of the president? "Nothing—disgust maybe. These people are destroying my country. They're stealing oil money, demolishing monuments, polluting nature reserves, building up the coast. People who can skip the three-year draft and just write a letter." Walid explained why he avoided Western journalists. He played in a band, and a year ago a reporter from the *Los Angeles Times* had interviewed him for an article. "We were over the moon," Walid said with a self-deprecating smile. "It was going to be our breakthrough in America! After playing, we got plastered, and then we made jokes about *Jurassic Park*, which is what we call the regime. He quoted that, and not a word about our music. Yep, then the secret services called. I had to report to them every day for weeks. Always the same questions, and hours of waiting. Boring, boring, boring. Why was I making Western music? Why was I going to Internet cafés? As if that was deviant behavior! Those motherfuckers have no idea what the world's like outside Syria. They're boring us to death, literally."

The waiter brought us more beers. Four moustachioed men in leather jackets came in and went to sit at the front table nearest to the dancing girls. Further up in the street, the most important "investigation facility" was located—it was obvious that the moustaches worked there. So that must be how you wind down after a hard day's work putting electric cattle prods up people's bottoms. How did the moustaches' wives explain that to their children? Uncle Mohammed is a teacher, Uncle Yasser is an engineer, and Papa tortures enemies of the president. "Tell me something positive," I said after yet another beer.

Walid's response was to tell me about a neighbor who had had an enormous wall built around his garden. "The whole neighborhood went mad and called in their connections. A few days later, a colonel came along, but he was too late. The neighbor had painted a colossal portrait of the president on the wall and *Yes-Yes-Yes President Assad For Ever!* The colonel was powerless to do anything about it."

I learned the most about dictatorships from Western expats. They were high up in the pecking order, the regimes couldn't do much to them, and many of them liked a drink, which made talking easier. At one dinner party, a European Union consultant told me that he'd been going to help the Lebanese government with "transparency." The idea was to list on the Internet all the documents that civilians might need to have whenever they had to seek approval for plans or projects. Civil servants had sabotaged the plan immediately, the consultant said. As long as citizens didn't know exactly which documents to take with them, the civil servants could carry on making up new requirements and saying "Come back tomorrow" until the citizens reached for their wallets.

During an Arab summit meeting, I got to know Gerhard, a German manager of a five-star hotel. A few hours before the summit, a man from the security services had come in—did Gerhard want to sign for 150 Egyptian tricolors? "I thought I was supposed to hang them up somewhere," the inebriated Gerhard recounted. "But suddenly there were three vans in front of the door, and I had to release 150 employees so they could go and cheer the president as he came down the street. I had a hotel full of guests for the summit, and not a single member of staff."

More power to alcohol, I would often think to myself—and even more so when I bumped into Roland's Dutch colleague from the Fayum oasis water company at a drinks party for the Dutch community in Cairo. He'd told me earlier that the ministries of irrigation and construction had sabotaged the project.

Now, after a refreshing number of half-pints of Saqqara beer, he continued. "The problem is the words. We say 'ministry' because the regime uses that word, but actually it's something quite different. A ministry isn't set up here to make irrigation more efficient and less corrupt; rather, it's to buy the support of thousands of farmers with offers of land, water, and fertilizer. In exchange, these farmers keep other farmers in check, and they all go out and cheer on the streets when the president or a minister comes to visit. At the same time, a ministry like this keeps thousands and thousands of Egyptians in the cities in work. The ministries here would function better if they sent eight civil servants home, and had two of them work for the salary of ten. Those two would earn enough for their family's keep. But then you've got eight people on the street. What are they going to do? That's right, the system is corrupt. But it goes further than that—the system is corruption itself. You have ten people doing not very much for a much-too-low salary—so low that they can't live on it, but too much for them to revolt. You keep them complicit and vulnerable that way, which means you've got them under control."

This story put me on the right track: A dictatorship is a fundamentally different system, but this is hidden from view because the Western media and specialists write about dictatorships as if they were writing about democracies. Egypt's dictator is called "President," even though he inherited his job from his predecessor who, in turn, used force to gain power. This particular dictator leads the "National Democratic Party," which is neither democratic nor a party. Egyptians often go to vote, but can you call them elections if you're not allowed to set up a party, can't run an open campaign, have no access to the state press, and have to vote under surveillance—which is still heavily defrauded afterwards?

Thanks to Saddam Hussein, it finally sunk in properly. In his country, I didn't just see the dictatorship; I *felt* it. Compare it with sex: You can read all you want, but until you do it, you really haven't got a clue what people keep going on about.

Iraq under Saddam was not only the most hardcore of all the Arab dictatorships; it was almost entirely isolated on the international stage, for since 1990 the country had endured the heaviest trade sanctions in history. Saddam didn't care about his image—tourists and investors weren't allowed in—

and Western correspondents had no special status. The result was that Iraq was the only Arab country in which a Western journalist was treated just like the next man.

It began with the visa. I'd faxed and telephoned Baghdad for months on end, and I'd stockpiled frequent-flyer points with futile flights between Cairo and Amman. The one time I did finally get through to Baghdad, they said, "We sent off the approval ages ago, mate. Get yourself to Amman." There I was told, "Tomorrow. Maybe." Finally, other journalists helped me hire a dodgy Egyptian with connections who could sort me out with a visa for a thousand crisp *Volkskrant* dollars. "Now we're there," he told me two weeks later. "The approval had been in the system for weeks—it just took me a while to find out who you have to bribe."

The visa was there. I just had to pay a bribe—another word that I'd never used in a sentence together with "I" before my time in the Middle East. Now I was getting a crash course: You put a bank note from the American Federal Reserve (in this case, one hundred dollars) into the envelope with your visa application. The functionary would nod that he'd seen the green note, and that'd be your receipt.

There was something intimate about bribery, but I'd soon had enough of it. "AIDS test," the customs officer on the Jordan–Iraqi border said—Iraq needed to protect itself against Western illnesses. For fifty dollars, though, they could do without it. "Wait here until we've finished the paperwork," another customs officer, sitting beneath a board reading SADDAM HUSSEIN, A WONDERFUL LEADER FOR A WONDERFUL PEOPLE, told us. My driver nodded; this was the moment to give the official his twenty-five dollars so that he'd stamp things now and not in one and a half hours. "Satellite telephone," said another official, while he went through my baggage. This would be a permit that I could obtain from the Ministry of Information for a pile of cash. We handed out more cigarettes, fizzy drinks, and money. Each obstacle had its price, and the way in which the customs officers indicated that they wanted money was by announcing, "We need to drink tea."

Finally, the road to Baghdad was open, and we tore through the desert for which the word "desolate" must have been invented. After five hours, the city of one thousand-and-one nights loomed into view. We drove past the *Suq Al-Har-amiya*, "the thieves market," where stolen loot from Kuwait was sold on, and under the victory arch that Saddam Hussein had originally wanted to grace with the skulls of dead Iranian soldiers rather than with their helmets. Past the Ministry of Defense, too; I'd done my research, so I knew that this was where the dictator Qasim had lain sleeping one day in 1963 when he was bombed by his own air force, arrested, and executed by his own soldiers. Reuters had sent a telegram offering forty thousand dollars for pictures of the corpse, but the coup organizers had turned them down.

We arrived at the Rashid hotel, and that's where I really started to feel what it was like to be in a system where you have no rights. The telephone switchboard operator would only put through calls if you paid him; and unless I paid off the guard in charge of the safes, he'd nick my equipment, too. The porter threw an aggrieved glance at the dollar note just handed to him, and looked at my sweating face. "You have more?" he asked. He knew that I knew he had a key to the room, and that he could steal everything when I went out. That's why they had safes, but I could not put my shoes, toothbrush, and water supplies in there. So I had to bribe the maids, the security, the cleaners, and anyone else who had access to my room.

The next morning, I made my compulsory visit to the Ministry of Information, and made the acquaintance of Mazjdi of the secret police. Every foreign journalist gets one of these agents. We call them "minders"—that way, it doesn't sound so bad. A little while later, there I was with my notebook, sitting down with the female director of the Saddam Hussein Cultural Center. I'd started by having a row with Mazjdi because I really didn't want to go to the Cultural Center, and after that I'd politely inspected five hundred portraits by twenty different artists, all of the same man. Now the three of us were sitting drinking tea, and I asked the director why the artists had only painted Saddam Hussein. She was a pale woman in her mid-forties who spoke broken English. "Are you crazy?" she cried. "How can you doubt our love for our leader, Mister President Saddam Hussein? There's a worldwide conspiracy against Iraq! What more fitting a subject for an artist's inspiration than our leader, may Allah protect him?"

Mazjdi beckoned me. He really wanted to move on to the Amariya shelter, where an American bomb had killed 403 Iraqis during the first Gulf War. "All Western journalists go to Amariya. It's an important story, or don't you want to tell the Dutch people about the war crimes the Americans are guilty of?"

In the car we'd already argued because I wanted to go to a primary school instead; there's no better window on the soul than children's drawings. But permission for such a visit remained impossible to get, and no one could explain why.

It went on like this for thirteen days, and by that time I was truly down and out. I'd always left other Arab countries with regret because there seemed so much more to do. I left Iraq a day early, despite all the hassles I'd gone through to get the visa. What a nightmare those thirteen days were, seeing people duck out of even the most innocent questions with comments like, "Iraq is blessed with such a strong leader as Mister President Saddam Hussein, may Allah preserve him." Or, "I'm certain that our leader has a solution for this." Or, "I'm not interested in politics." I spent all day sitting in the car with a secret agent who had God-knows-what on his conscience, but with whom I had to dine out every evening—on the *Volkskrant* expense account, naturally.

"Amazing that they have Dutch beer here, Mazjdi."

"Thanks to Saddam Hussein, we have everything."

In the hotel, I felt like a walking cash machine. Every evening, I had to take into account the fact that my drinking water could be stolen, and my clothes and my notes. The phone in my room was bugged, everything on the television was about Saddam, and apparently there were hidden cameras behind the full-length mirrors in my room. "A real man drops his trousers," my colleagues had sworn to me when we'd met in the whisky bar in Amman for a few courage-building drinks before my departure.

I ordered a taxi for the next morning because in the evenings the route to the border was controlled by bandits who shared their booty with the police. I packed my bags and, late that evening, walked over to the nearby Ministry of Information for the fleecing that would end my stay: One hundred dollars per day spent in Iraq, another hundred for having a satellite telephone, and fifty dollars a day for Mazjdi. They even gave me a stamped receipt because Western accountants are so strict . . . As I took my leave, the director said, "You've now checked out."

"Ordinary Arabs have an expression for this," the Jordanian driver told me once we'd left Iraq. "*Hamiha haramiha*—he who protects you, robs you."

I was shattered after that trip. Once I'd recovered in Cairo, I realized that it wasn't normal fear that had made such an impression on me. I'd had to deal with that fear in Libya and Syria, too—and, if I asked enough questions, in any Arab dictatorship. What had had such an effect on me in Iraq was my own vulnerability, the humiliating powerlessness I'd experienced at the embassy in Amman, at the border, in the Rashid hotel, and at the greedy Ministry of Information. I had been permanently watched, and had suffered from the constant realization that I would have no rights if I was robbed. I could have disappeared without a trace, and no one would have blinked.

This was dictatorship in its naked form, and I had to physically experience it in order to understand how fundamentally different such a system is from democracy. If someone breaks the law in the Netherlands and harms me, I know I can go to the police about it. If they don't do anything, I can apply pressure higher up or go to the civil commissioner. I can get a lawyer, go to the press, or go to an MP or the European Court. There are many different authorities I can turn to in the exercise of my civil rights, and these different bodies monitor and correct each other. This makes the abuse of power and corruption more difficult, and at least you have the illusion of legal certainty—the basis of democracy. When I see a police officer in the Netherlands, I relax because that man or woman is there for me. When an Arab sees a police officer, he starts running. *Hamiha haramiha.*

Of course, not everyone in Iraq is corrupt or terrified; just like in Western democracies, things don't always work to the system's dictates. Every Arab country has its own variant, and Arabs don't spend the whole day being robbed, accused, or grassed on. But if something does happen to you, there are no universal procedures for enforcing your rights. This makes you vulnerable, and that's why my minder Mazjdi got into a panic when I wanted to deviate from the program. It would have made him susceptible to blackmail—"Where did you disappear to all that time with that Western spy?" And Mazjdi, in turn, was probably blackmailing his subordinates.

***

Some time after that trip to Iraq, I briefly returned to the Netherlands for what we called "the correspondent days," a biennial event during which correspondents returned home for a week. That's where the penny finally dropped. The meeting began pleasantly, because correspondents are pleasant people, and I relaxed even more when I discovered that many people shared my uneasiness about the news agencies. Our men and women in our London, Paris, Berlin, and Washington bureaus all felt that the wrong topics were dominating the news, and that we were following the news agencies too slavishly.

This was balm to my soul, but were we talking about the same frustrations? That evening, at the drinks session, a colleague stationed in a Western country asked me what kind of people the Arabs were. I'd worked out a standard answer for that one: I adopted my specialist's voice, and said that the Arab world was extremely varied and that Egypt was the only country I knew well. I rarely spoke to women, so my impressions only related to half of the people; and even then, if I'd gotten to know around one person each day, in three years that amounted to around one thousand people. Out of 260 million Arabs, that was 0.0004 percent of the population.

Yeah, yeah, she reacted—now say what you really think. And then it hit me: I didn't know what Arabs were like, not because I wasn't trying, but because I *couldn't* know.

"You work in a democracy," I said to my colleague, "and in that kind of system you've got all kinds of instruments you can use to double-check your impressions of the 0.0001 percent of the people you talk to. There's a context. People in your country dare to talk to you. They dare to talk to each other, and there's freedom of the press. There are opinion polls, TV and radio ratings, election results. In other words, in your situation, the news agencies can illuminate a much greater part of society, and you can investigate things for yourself. The articles you write might be drowned out by the news agencies, and that's what you're fed up with. But in a dictatorship the problem is of a different kind. There's no way I can come up with my own stuff. Where you are, opposition parties, NGOs, action groups, or journalists can call the leader to task, and he has to defend himself. Where I am, the leader sends in a gang of thugs. Knowledge is power: Dictators try to gain total power, which means doing everything to prevent their subjects getting hold of any information. The more opaque the society, the easier it is to corrupt and abuse power, and the harder it is for an opposition to form.

"The fact that you're not afraid to listen to me telling you this, and I'm not afraid to say it, is the difference between dictatorship and democracy. Imagine if we knew that half of us here at this table—although we don't know who they are—

have got to be working for the secret services. And what if all our bosses were party members, and reported our thoughts to the secret services? Don't you think we'd all shut up?"

When I went to Cairo as a correspondent, journalistic practice seemed a set of tools you could unpack and use all over the world. But dictatorships and democracies weren't two cars of different makes. If a democracy is a car, a dictatorship is a cow or a horse. The man who turns up with a screwdriver or a soldering iron is powerless.

Chapter Five

All the News That's Fit to Print

My third year as a correspondent went by, and the world seemed stranger every day. Syria banned the Disney hit *The Lion King* because the president was called Assad, which means lion in Arabic. In Saudi Arabia, *The Pink Panther* was called *The Pink Hyena* because panther is *fahd*, and that was the king's name. President Mubarak was voted "Man of the Year" by all the Egyptian daily, weekly, and monthly papers. In the days before the Iraqi "referendum," people didn't get a dialing tone when they picked up the phone, but a recorded message with "Yes! Yes! Yes! Saddam."

No wonder people told each other jokes in abundance: "Congratulations, Mr. President!" the advisor says. "99.98 percent voted for you at the referendum. That means that only

0.02 percent were against you. What more do you want?"
The leader growls, "Their names."

Burglars break into the safe at the central bank. There's
a big panic until the governor comes out and says in relief,
"False alarm. Nothing important was stolen—only the results
of the 2015 election."

The most surreal thing was my own job. Student riots
broke out in Iran, and I had to cover them from Cairo
because Tehran kept its gates closed. How many readers
and listeners would know that I couldn't even place a direct
phone call to Iran from Egypt, and that Cairo was about the
least-suitable place on earth from where to follow these dis-
turbances? Not many, I hoped, and it really couldn't come
out that I knew precisely six words of Persian.

Syria was closed off at that time, too; despite my barrage of
faxes ("Your country deserves to be described from the inside,
not by my colleague in Tel Aviv"), I never got a personal visa.
Other journalists had the same problem, and the Cairo Foreign Press Association organized a very brief and tightly run
group trip to Damascus. Part of this was a collective interview with the Syrian minister of economic affairs, for which
our opening question was: "Each year, two hundred thousand
young Syrians flood into the work market. How is Syria going
to help them find a job?" The minister smiled sympatheti-
cally and said, "Thanks to the wise leadership of our president, we don't have any unemployment. At the most, just a
few lazy people." It went on like this for half an hour; then, as
I was leaving the ministry at the end, a pretty young woman
grabbed hold of me. Did I belong to the group of Western
journalists who'd been invited by the Ministry of Information

to come and look into the impressive progress of Syria under the leadership of President Hafez Al-Assad? She'd seen us on the news. Could I pass on this petition to the minister and have it signed? Her brother would pick it up later that evening from my hotel because, of course, a nice girl like her couldn't come to me. Was this an appeal for a pardon for a group of political prisoners? A complaint against human rights crimes? A plea for democracy? Our entire group would be thrown out of the country and my name put at the top of the blackest of black lists if I handed a petition like that in. But then I took another look. It was an appeal for a job in television. "I want to be a presenter," she smiled charmingly.

I sometimes imagined I was taking part in a reality-TV show where participants were given impossible assignments. Mine was to play a journalist in a system where good journalism is a contradiction in terms. It produced some droll images, but the worse the dictatorship, the less funny it became.

A little less than a year after I'd arrived, the Cairo Foreign Press Association arranged a group trip to Iraq via the Ministry of Information in Baghdad. It was complete madness. The secret-service minders practically sat on our laps. They'd regularly leave us waiting in lobbies for hours on end without any explanation, and then shove us into taxis for an excursion. Slipping away wasn't possible because then you'd put people in danger. If an Iraqi saw his neighbor (whom he'd hated for years) chatting to a Westerner, he might make a call to his "friend" in the secret services: "My neighbor has been recruited by a spy." Could the neighbor prove his innocence? And to which authorities? Perhaps that sly journalist from *Hulanda* was an informant or agent provocateur himself? You do hear such funny things; and if he was an agitator and you didn't report him immediately, he might report you.

Part of the trip was an excursion to the south, thirty or so of us in a bus, leading to unavoidable jokes about school trips. Soon, everybody was playing I Spy—". . . an absurd wall painting of the Leader." There was a portrait of Saddam wearing a black toga in front of the Law Courts. Then he was in front of a five-star hotel, wearing a Hawaiian shirt and smoking a Cuban cigar; in front of a print shop, dressed as a tourist with a big camera dangling over his beer belly; in uniform next to some barracks; and outside an adventure park, against a backdrop of snow, forests, and mountains, dressed as an Alpine hunter, complete with silly hat.

In Kerbala, the fun stopped. At the world famous Al-Abbas mosque, we were guided around a small museum that the regime had set up to commemorate the victims of the 1991 uprising. Shiites had tried to topple Saddam's regime, and had been quickly and ruthlessly put down. The dead being remembered were supporters of the regime who had been chopped to pieces by the rebels at the beginning of the uprising. We saw authentic nooses, a meat hook, dried-up pools of blood displayed behind glass, and pictures of children's heads that, according to the minders, had been hacked off by "agents from the other side of the fence": Iran. The museum was on every school trip's itinerary.

There we were, guardians of free speech, listening to the keeper of the Syed Madhi Fadhil al-Ghurabi mosque after having carefully written down his name. Al-Ghurabi with a G-H cleared his throat and said, in classical Arabic, translated by one of our minders, "Our Leader, Mr. Saddam Hussein, may Allah protect him, has set aside fifteen kilos of gold, and 150 kilos of silver, for the restorations, despite the continuing aggression against Iraq by Iran and the West." On the wall there was a picture of a praying Saddam, and a family tree proving that the Leader was a descendant of the Prophet Mohammed. The late King Hussain of Jordan, also a relative, had had this family history "researched" by scripture scholars. Al-Ghurabli looked at the minders—was his rendition alright?

We'd been told that we could ask questions, and some thought it was worth trying. Was it true that, while putting down the uprising, random civilians were tied to tanks so that the rebels wouldn't shoot at them? That the Friday afternoon sermon hadn't been held for years because the regime was afraid of gatherings? Under the shadow of the meat hook, Al-Ghurabi began to pour with sweat, and the minders quickly ended the talk.

They led us on to the Saddam Hussein hospital—you didn't need a notebook to remember the names of the institutions in Iraq. A photographer in our group had been coming to Iraq every six months for years, and recognized one of the doctors from previous visits.

"Good to see you! How is the hospital?"

"*Alhamdulillah*, God is great, as we say."

Nearly all the equipment on the ward was broken, and spare parts couldn't be obtained because of the sanctions. At least that's what the regime said. Another doctor explained that all the cancer patients had to be sent home because there was no money for medicine; with a glance at the bored but happily nodding minders, he continued angrily, saying that the sanctions had turned Iraq into a refugee camp. "And why? Because Iraq is supposed to be harboring weapons of mass destruction. Everyone knows that we haven't had those weapons for a long time and that America just wants to destroy Iraq, don't they?"

A German journalist from our group decided to act as

if we were in a democracy. He pointed out that, in the area where the top party leaders lived, he'd seen a swimming pool installed, as well as Mercedes cars and satellite dishes . . . The regime had money for that, didn't it? The doctor faltered, Oxford accent and all. "I'm certain our worthy president has a plan to break the back of this crisis," he said. And then he was gone.

"Have you got your quotes?" the head minder asked. We nodded, and then we were gone, too.

This was dictatorship laid bare again. I quickly came up with a background story entitled, "Angst rules in Kerbala." But is that what came across? If it had taken me so long to see through dictatorship, what would it be like for readers living in the safe Netherlands?

In any case, the boss gave me his compliments on a different piece. The Minister of Foreign Affairs, Tareq Aziz, had been able to make time for us because we'd been a group. It had been a stage play with standard answers to standard questions—sanctions, UN resolutions, diplomatic maneuvers . . . For anyone who kept up with the news agencies, nothing new was said. But Tareq Aziz was a famous name, so I'd scored. But a couple of reactions stayed with me. Someone from head office asked why I hadn't been able to get a visa more quickly, and one editor was annoyed that I hadn't responded to his urgent email. "Didn't you know I was in Iraq?" I answered.

"Yes, and . . .?"

At which point, I had to spell out the fact that you can't send emails in a country where fear rules. It was rather embarrassing, but I couldn't reproach my colleagues too much, because they'd based their ideas partly on my work. In two years, I'd made the front page ten times, I'd written hundreds of articles, and had been on the radio at least two hundred times, but the reality of dictatorship was pretty much only apparent in my subordinate clauses. And, for the sake of clarity, I'd continued to use the word "president" instead of "head crook"; "parliament" instead of "applause machine"; and "commentator" instead of "inciter," "goad," or "arse-licker."

Then, one day, Egypt hit the news again. European and African heads of state were coming to Cairo for the first Euro–African summit—an attempt by the Egyptian regime to act as a "bridge between the continents." The city creaked under the security measures, and I was happy because "my" area had been out of the news cycle for a while. But that happiness was to be short-lived.

Just before the opening, all of the journalists were brought together in a room in the Cairo Conference Center. Our mobile telephones were confiscated, and we were told that we wouldn't be able to leave until the closing address. The journalists who'd flown in from Europe were the most furious, but protest was futile.

There we sat, and I felt like yelling out, "What are we doing here while a band of crooks is bleeding this country dry?" Later that day, the European and African leaders would feed us their great quotes, which we would have forgotten before we'd even broadcast them. Imagine if a people's uprising had happened right outside the door. The correspondents would all have chimed, "Nobody expected this." But why would nobody have expected this? Because we'd had other notions, or because we only looked at what the news agencies had indicated was "the story?"

I had already abandoned the idea that you would know what was going on in the world if you followed the news. But now, in the Cairo Conference Center, I realized that the most important element was missing from the news about the Middle East. A dictatorship is not an obstacle to good journalism in the same category as, say, the routine incompetence of travel agencies that drives you crazy. Dictatorship itself was the most important thing to report about in the Arab world. In some countries, it was harder to see just how dreadful it was through the thick clouds of propaganda and misinformation, but in essence all of the twenty Arab dictatorships were set up in the same way. Writing "around" this was like reporting on France or the Netherlands in 1943 without mentioning the occupation. In reportage, analysis, and cross-talk, I now felt, you should first highlight the dictatorship, and only then talk about the exceptional events— the news.

Locked up in the Cairo Conference Center, I decided to change course and from then on to cover everyday life in a dictatorship as a central part of my work. Over the ensuing months, I discovered just how difficult that was.

The problem lay in the basic principles of quality journalism. People watch the news, listen to the radio, and read the papers because they want to understand more about the world. What they read and see has to be correct. That's why you need a first name, a last name, both sides of the story, proper checking, and double-checking—you need verifiable information. As *The New York Times* boasts on its front page: "All the News That's Fit to Print." In a democracy, it's an extremely useful and lovely principle. But in a dictatorship, only a minuscule part of reality is verifiable and fit to print; the rest gets stuck in four big filters.

The first filter is fear within the resident population, which prevents correspondents from finding out very much at all. As an Iraqi girl said to the BBC after the fall of Baghdad years later, her life under Saddam was "like having someone inside your head checking every time you wanted to say anything, whether it was risky or not."

The fear differed from country to country; but even when smoke-screen-free or brave people told me things, I couldn't get any further because I couldn't check anything. There were virtually no reliable and verifiable figures or statistics against which I could set these cases in a broader perspective—which was the second filter.

But newspapers also have background or feature sections where correspondents can air their views, don't they? It's true that I could get some things off my chest there; but that also had its limitations, and the best stories in particular stayed out of shot. When I decided to write a background article about the vulnerability and powerlessness of ordinary people, I realized it was only worth doing if I could give an example that would touch readers' hearts. So, in one instance, I scrolled through my files and came up with a Dutch woman living in Baghdad—she would let readers feel what dictatorship was like.

She was one of the last remaining Dutch people in Baghdad; I had met her on my first trip to Iraq. Due to the sanctions, there was no Dutch embassy in Baghdad, so the consul in Amman had given me her number. He told me that she was an old lady who had married an Iraqi Christian in the early 1950s. She hadn't left Iraq for decades, and still spoke Dutch like the Queen. At first, she refused to meet me.

"We don't associate with Catholics," she said tartly down the telephone, and she clearly only half-believed me when I told her that *de Volkskrant* had swapped its Catholic colors for a more progressive outlook before I'd even been born. Eventually, she agreed, and a few hours later we were standing outside her house in the rain. A shutter opened and I stepped forward, but the door remained closed. My minder, Mazjdi from the Ministry of Information, looked at me, and I looked at him. We were in an area that obviously used to be quite well to do, with nice trellis-work and an expansive but empty garden.

Finally, the door opened and an awkward greeting ensued. She probably hadn't dared to turn me down. We were offered a glass of lemonade, and Mazjdi leafed through a few magazines. I had told him that I was conveying the best wishes of the embassy, and he didn't mind us speaking Dutch. The old lady began to tell me that she couldn't leave the country because the regime was asking for twenty thousand dollars per exit visa. Her husband was ill, and the necessary medicines weren't available. Her own heart problems were simple to treat in the Netherlands but not in Iraq, so she'd been served a death sentence.

Because Saddam Hussein refused to cooperate with weapons inspectors, Iraq could not trade. In order to prevent the country from starving, it was allowed to export oil, with the income being controlled by the UN—the so-called Oil for Food program. Did she have enough to eat? Without betraying any emotion, the lady explained that everyone in the neighborhood received the food distribution correctly, at least until the UN functionary left—if he turned up in the first place. If he wasn't there, everyone handed everything back in, and the regime's offices had first choice. The rest went to the most loyal families, and the other neighbors had to go and beg from them. I talked about the Netherlands for a while, but she clearly wanted to get rid of us. One last thing then: Why had the front door remained closed for so long? She nodded icily at Mazjdi. "You didn't say you were bringing him. He was on the television recently. Secret service, high up. My seventeen-year-old granddaughter is staying here. If he sees her, he'll come back later to . . . you understand? First, I had to let her escape through the back door."

That was dictatorship. By Allah, how I wanted to use this story. I'd got it reasonably fact-checked, but then Mazjdi handed me over to another minder for a day. He was a former ambassador who'd returned to the Ministry of Information and had been working for a Japanese correspondent for years. They trusted one another, the Japanese correspondent trusted me, and so we could talk. I discussed the Dutch lady in veiled terms. "She certainly won't have exaggerated," he said decisively. "That's why so many people become informants, and why every father sends one son into the army. That's how you build up connections, in case you get into trouble."

I had no reason to mistrust the former ambassador, but the old woman didn't make my article. I felt there was too much of a risk that Mazjdi would find out about it, either through a Dutch Iraqi or through the embassy. The woman has since died.

One of my beer-drinking partners in Cairo was Gie, a Flemish man who managed a sweet factory for a multinational. "I wanted to import eight tons of a special oil," he once told me. "I couldn't find out anywhere what the requirements for such a container of oil would be. The ministries of environment, transport, economic affairs, and health all told different stories, and no one returned my calls. However, my factory couldn't continue manufacturing without this oil, so I imported it. The container hadn't even got to the harbor when it was seized—the oil had to be destroyed or redistributed, and it was going to cost me sixty thousand dollars. I called my lawyer, who called a contact, who called another contact. I ended up paying a 'consultant' six hundred dollars for 'legal advice,' and my oil was allowed through customs. I've got a special little chap who will go to prison for me if we get caught. Any Western companies who say they don't operate through bribery in Egypt are liars. If they didn't, they'd have gone bankrupt long ago."

Gie's problems illustrated beautifully how corruption and mismanagement wreck a country's economy. Yet the story didn't find its way into the economic supplement because I didn't want to put Gie's career at risk, and the Egyptian embassy in The Hague reads everything—which is why, in reality, Gie has a different name and isn't Flemish.

The vulnerability of the sources was a third filter that kept the realities of daily life under a dictatorship out of the news. And there was a fourth one. Sometimes I'd hear something, I'd have it fact-checked, and I'd have sources with first and last names . . . but then it wouldn't be news. One example was the traffic mortality rate in the Middle East. Because of the poor state of the roads in the region, the clapped-out cars, the corrupt police, and the useless hospitals, an Arab is fifty times more likely to have a fatal car accident than a European. It's a bloodbath in the Arab world—day in, day out. In this instance, the usual impediments to getting a good story don't exist: There are figures available, you can get great quotes from UN press guys, and the names and last names of the victims and their relatives are not that important for the human angle. So I waited for an exceptionally big accident on the Cairo to Alexandria motorway, and grafted my story onto it.

So then I had the one article . . . but that's as far as it went. How was it possible that the biggest bloodbath in the Arab world was only good for one piece?

The answer was, once again, because Arab lands are not democracies. Compare them with the Netherlands. While I was in the Middle East, an increasing number of my countrymen were concluding that mass immigration cost more than it delivered. A certain person offered that opinion, it received media coverage, and when his message got hold he was invited to speak more often. This inspired supporters to write in, hold demonstrations, and organize events; in this way, resistance to further immigration made it onto the political agenda. It took time because, even in a democracy, the elite can keep certain issues off the agenda. But sooner or later the issues come to the surface, and that's precisely the difference between ours and a closed system such as a dictatorship. The mainstream Arab media will never report that, "Today, thousands of Egyptians hit the streets to protest against the president's appointment of his half-illiterate brother as government advisor." No, and neither would they report: "Today, the secretary of traffic safety in Egypt has given a petition containing 3 million signatures to the president and asked him to act against the children of generals and politicians responsible for 200kph hit-and-run accidents."

If something deviates from the everyday, and verifiable information is available, it can become news. But, to remain news, an issue has to have legs; it must stay in motion. "We're following this story closely," they say on CNN; but without development there's nothing to follow. That's why the hunger in Wau in Sudan was not a story for the editors: "Oh, no, not another conflict with no end in sight."

***

I once asked a TV colleague back at the studios what he thought the news was. He gave an embarrassed grin: "If it bleeds, it leads. We like to open with attacks, kidnaps, murders, and large, bloody accidents, because they grab the public's attention. You also have to divide the number of deaths by the number of kilometers from the studios back home. Dead whites are bigger news than dead blacks or Asians, and dead Christians are bigger news than dead people of other faiths—except that, as American colleagues pun: Jews are news. So an attack in Jerusalem could make the headlines, but a small bomb in Algiers or Delhi won't make the broadcast."

The jokes were charmingly cynical and became something of a running gag. But they also seemed to have a function, specifically to reiterate that nobody knows exactly why something becomes news. You can list the requirements for something to be news, but why it actually makes the news programs . . . The only certainty for journalists in the West is that if something really important happens, sooner or later ordinary people will make themselves heard.

That's the West, but in dictatorships people are oppressed. Protesting and getting things on the agenda are impossible, and so much remains out of shot—not only everyday life, but also things that have a huge effect on people's lives. In Egypt, 75 million people live in a residential area the size of the Netherlands, and each year the population increases by 1.5

million. In order to keep up with this population explosion, the authorities need to create five hundred thousand new jobs a year, build one hundred thousand new houses, ten thousand new schools, one thousand new centers of higher education, one hundred new hospitals, and a handful of new universities . . . This is how much pressure population growth creates—not only in Egypt, but also in Yemen, Syria, and other Arab countries. That's 6 million more people every year, and when there's no water or work for them they may very well decide to come to Europe. But until they do that in their masses, the population explosion is not news:

A further sixteen thousand Arabs were born today
By our correspondent

CAIRO—Today the population in Arab countries, just like yesterday and the day before, grew by sixteen thousand people . . .

Neither traffic deaths nor population growth were news, but at least there were statistics about them. By contrast, nobody knows how many Egyptian girls have their vulvas mutilated annually—"female circumcision," they call it. Nor do we know how many people in the Arab world have been locked away without a fair trial (or a trial of any kind). Nor how many billions of skimmed dollars various generals have managed to secrete in foreign accounts. And there's no chance of finding out how many Arabs are killed or handicapped each year by such criminal mismanagement. Nobody knows, and nobody dares to protest about it.

An Egyptian doctor friend told me about the chaos and corruption in the hospitals. Doctors were committing fatal errors because their qualifications hadn't been acquired through exams, but bribes; patients had to bribe doctors to receive treatment; corrupt buyers bought too-expensive medicines or the wrong ones in exchange for fat commission fees. *That's what I'm going to write about*, I thought enthusiastically. But there were no figures about damage, waste, and bribery, and that doctor could, at the limit, only be quoted anonymously in the paper. In the West, the victims of such a system would set up a Patients Association; but, like the wife of that doctor said, "The only time I've voted freely in my life was on Idols. And I swear to you, if I set up a fan club for my idol, I'd have the secret service on my back."

This was journalism in a dictatorship, but how could it be any different? You can't fill a radio news program or a newspaper with personal impressions and anecdotes that you don't even know to be true, or at all representative. That's why those colleagues who spoke really good Arabic and had more experience and contacts than I did stuck to the news stream from the news agencies. And that's why even the most brutal dictators didn't deport those news agencies. They didn't need to, because the agencies had already put on their own gags.

It was as simple as that, and that's why so much remained out of sight and why you had to start from scratch when people suddenly did want to know more about the Arabs. Like after September 11, 2001.

Chapter Six

September 11 and the Blank Spots in the Dictatorship

It's hard to imagine now but, before my appointment in 1998, *de Volkskrant* had had serious discussions over whether having a correspondent in the Arab world was still necessary. Couldn't it be covered from Israel? At the end of the 1990s few were concerned about Islam, and the peace process between Israel and Palestine seemed to be limping towards a resolution. Once there was peace at last, the Arabs would climb aboard the democratic bandwagon, along with the rest of humanity. "The end of history," it was called at the time, and a columnist grumbled that everyone was starting to look like everyone else: "The world is going to be one giant McDonald's."

95

It's all part of the game, but in that climate my observations to my bosses about our distorted representation of Arabs had little effect. To them, the Arab world was on the same rung as Latin America on the ladder: One page-long background article once in a while was enough.

I was stuck with it. Because you can hardly squeeze anything out of it, a dictatorship is like a map with uncharted areas. During quiet periods, correspondents can talk around these blank spots by limiting their reporting to events for which there is verifiable information: Summits, diplomatic breakthroughs, bombings. But when something big happens, the public wants to know things that the correspondent can't find out. What do you do then? There's competition in the news industry, too—not only between domestic and foreign news, but also between correspondents who want to get their own area on the front page, or who covet someone else's job or travel budget. When you're asked what's going on in your area, it's not a good idea if you reply, "It's hard to know." You run the risk of the editor-in-chief looking at you during the next round of cutbacks. Why should we invest in you if you never know anything?

This dilemma was brought into sharp relief when the Syrian dictator Hafez Al-Assad died. Suddenly, Syria hit the headlines, and the gates of Damascus sprung wide open. The world news caravan was on the move, and I'd hardly left the arrivals hall when I was set to work. "Our correspondent has arrived in Damascus. What is the atmosphere there?" As if I knew, so I hid behind a wall of trivial facts, like all the other journalists did: The procession will go this way, the burial will be there on that day, President

A will be attending but Leader B will not, there will be x number of days of national morning . . . It would work a few times, but it was boring, and you could serve it up from the studio just as easily. When a leader who has ruled for this long dies, editors want to know more—as in, "What's going to happen now in Syria?"

And that was one of the blank spots. Assad would be succeeded by his son; that much was certain, but after that? It seemed to me that the regime wouldn't be rushing to share power with an opposition it had been repressing with an iron fist for decades. Damascus had been brought to a standstill by security measures, loudspeakers blared out the whole day, "Dear Assad, we support you with blood and soul," and the pinboards in the corridors of the Ministry of Information were decorated with sheets of paper reading: "General assembly tomorrow at 7:00 AM at the main entrance. Obligatory attendance for the funeral of Our Leader for Eternity." This wasn't exactly the sound of a new wind blowing, and the few Syrians I spoke to were mainly afraid of chaos. They'd rather see another strong man come into power than go through any risky experiments, they said.

What was going to happen in Syria? A successor is almost always weaker, because fewer people are indebted to him. He would be supported by the powers who'd supported his predecessor, but they'd only do that as long as their own pockets were being filled—and for that their own positions had to remain unthreatened. The possibility of a new wind was therefore limited, and why would a dictator want to hand over some of his power? Say he introduced democracy, and it went wrong and you had a coup. Who'd be first against the wall, along with his family? Not to mention the risk that would arise of being tried as a former dictator.

I think the correspondents should have said, "We don't know what the new leader or the people want. We *can't* know because it's a dictatorship." Then we could have explained what a dictatorship was, with the conclusion that one chief crook would probably be followed by another in Syria.

But the senior correspondents who'd been specially flown in by CNN or the BBC said something else, and so did I. We quoted the spokespersons who talked up the regime in their pitch-perfect English, and used words like "openness," "thaw," and "Damascan spring." We reported that critics, such as the aforementioned MP Riad Sef, would be free to act, and that the new leader had promised modernization, complete with Internet cafés, satellite dishes, and mobile telephones.

That's the way Syria was going, we suggested, making up a story that was remarkably similar to the ones at the funerals of the Moroccan King Hassan and the Jordanian King Hussein, in previous years. "For decades, this country has been ruled by the iron fist of the now deceased, a leader from the old school. He brought stability but also stagnation, and now the people can't wait for the reforms his son will bring. He belongs to the new generation, and these people are more familiar with the West. The only question is how much the leader will *dare* to do because some forces are against reform." As if dictatorship was a kind of misunderstanding that the successor would clear up, like replacing an incorrectly installed computer program.

The funeral, "with a massive turnout of people come to pay their last respects to the president," went ahead without incident, and the following day Syria went back to being on a par with Colombia in the news pecking order.

Then came September 11. Suddenly, in the words of one Saudi commentator, Arabs were "the dish of the day," and for the correspondents on the ground it was party time. It wasn't that we jumped up and down or admitted it to each other. Every profession has its taboos, but you didn't have to be an anthropologist to understand that celebrating a war or a bomb is just not done—despite the fact that we correspondents would be out of a job if there weren't any bombs or wars. The attacks meant that I'd get thousands of euros worth of extra commissions from the news department of NOS, the Dutch public broadcaster. The newspaper gave me a big travel budget and almost unlimited space, in prime spots and with excellent photographs. I was almost humming *Thank-You-Bin-La-den.*

But all of the excitement quickly gave way to frustration, because now correspondents were paying the price for their inadequate reporting of the Arab world over previous decades. How could my audience know that the Arab world was made up of dictatorships and that, in this kind of system, everything was different? The Western media had "covered" dictatorship, true, but only in supplements and documentaries. The suggestion had been that this kind of background information was optional and that you still could understand the Arab world if you followed just the news. But the news was always about the Arab League, violent incidents, and photo opportunities at events like the Euro-African summit.

The main question on September 12 was how much support Al-Qaida had. How big was the enemy and how afraid should the West be? Bin Laden had committed the attacks "in the name of Islam." If a 100 million Islamic Arabs supported this, the West could expect a colossal conflict.

Well, yeah. In Western countries you could get out the

opinion polls, and look at parliamentary acts and the opinion pages of the papers. But Arab "parliaments" and "papers" didn't deserve these appellations, and opinion polls didn't exist or were unreliable—in a dictatorship, who was going to say what he honestly thought to an anonymous voice over the phone?

The question of how many Muslims Bin Laden was speaking for couldn't be answered, but this was hard for correspondents to admit. So, like my fellow reporters, I simply had a go. I said that talk shows on Al-Jazeera were sympathetic towards Al-Qaida, and that famous Arabs from the entertainment industry were often extremely critical of America and that this didn't seem to affect their popularity. There were long-running productions of plays that were critical of the U.S., protest songs against Americans got to number one in the charts, and films with a negative depiction of the West were box-office hits.

It was guesswork. The more often I was asked about the popularity of Bin Laden, the more I was tempted to give an honest answer. I wanted to shout it on the radio, or write it in the newspaper in capital letters: "I Don't Know. I Can't Know. This is a Dictatorship."

I didn't do it. But what an advantage more openness would have brought. Correspondents would no longer have had to act like Arab know-it-alls, dodging around the blank spots of their knowledge. They would simply be able to say that things were different in a dictatorship, that you should remember that a human rights activist's salary was being paid by Western organizations when you heard them calling for "solidarity between East and West," and that the Arab scholar who called fundamentalism the main enemy was being watched by the secret police—that is, if he didn't work for them.

If correspondents had given more explanations and been more open about dictatorship, they might have been able to "decode" the great quotes coming out of the Arab world after 9/11. The same went for the images—for example, the angry men burning a flag and shouting, "America, Satan!" Certainly, in the aftermath of 9/11, these were frightening shots for Westerners, and even more so if they weren't put into context: Guys, you probably think that a demonstration is something citizens use freely to express whatever they are for or against, but in a dictatorship such "outbursts of anger" are often staged or are at least heavily managed by the regime. Many of the demonstrators work for the secret services or are, at the least, being closely watched by them. Bear in mind that Arab regimes can kill two birds with one stone with such mediagenic outbursts of anger. They give their subjects the impression that they are charting their own course and dare to stand up to the mighty America. At the same time, they are signaling to Western governments that this wound-up rabble might also be the boss-in-waiting—would you rather do business with them?

If correspondents in the Arab world had been open about their limited vision, we could have produced a different kind of reportage. It would have been possible to write an article saying, "I can't prove it and it might be nonsense, but it seems the dictators" propaganda within the education system and the state media has tremendous effect on ordinary Arabs, and they appear much more afraid of the West than of their own leaders. At least if I take a random Egyptian and ask him about his country's position in the world order, he'll mostly say something like, 'We're the cradle of civilization, our soldiers are amongst the best in the world, and the Suez Canal is the most important canal in the world. Egypt has got the Al-Azhar mosque and forms the bridge between Africa and Asia, between the Eastern and Western parts of the Arab world and Islam. Whoever controls Egypt controls the world, and that's why world powers are always trying to take us over.' In Iraq, even when people are out of their compatriots' earshot, they tell the following story, 'We have the oldest civilization, the most fertile land in the Middle East, and a lot of gas and oil. We are the hinge between the Turkish, Persian, and Arab worlds. Whoever controls us holds the world in their hands, and that's why the big powers are working against us.' And when I go to Syria, this is what I often hear: 'Our country also comprises what has become occupied Palestine, and we once had Lebanon, part of Jordan, and a province that Turkey stole from us. The real Syria is a world treasure, and that's why the big powers chopped us up into pieces and try to dominate us.'"

The words are different, but the refrain in every Arab dictatorship is the same: EVERYONE IS AGAINST US. It's banged into ordinary Arabs through the media and their education from a very young age, so don't expect them to be pro-Western. They might want to get rid of their dictators, but all they've heard about all the time is that there's a much greater threat beyond their borders—the West.

There was another advantage to greater transparency. If you said that there were blank spots in your knowledge, you could then explain how you got around them—what kind of compass you used to navigate the map of dictatorship. I would have loved to have been honest about my own presuppositions or, even better, my perspective. It had been formed during my year as a student in Egypt, when I'd almost casually asked my peers whether Islam was compatible with democracy and human rights. Their answers had varied widely: They aren't compatible, because Islam is Eastern and democracy is Western; they are, because Islam is the highest form of democracy; they aren't compatible, because you have your human rights and we have ours; they are compatible, because Islam is another word for democracy and human rights.

Everyone had their own interpretation, and could support it with a personal mixture of Koranic verses, the speeches of the Prophet, and historical examples. Who was right? At that time, you'd get top marks on your anthropology course if you answered "nobody." Unless you believed that one of those interpretations embodied God's will (and how were you going to fact-check that with God?), you'd have to come to the conclusion that "Islam" didn't exist. There were only interpretations, and it was all about who had the power to enforce his own interpretation as Holy Law. As a correspondent, I'd stuck with this view and—coincidentally—I'd also found confirmation that Muslims interpret their religion in many different ways. But who knows what I would have come home with if I'd presumed that Islam was in essence nonviolent or, indeed, intolerant?

***

It's easy to be wise after the event but, looking back, I don't think that the big Western media did a good job in the aftermath of 9/11. Not only did we fail to be honest about the fact that we simply couldn't know if Bin Laden had the support of ordinary Muslims, we also didn't address properly the second big question after the attacks: Why do they hate us?

The problem was already there in that word "hate." In the Western media, the battle with Al-Qaida was already a battle *against* Al-Qaida, like in a Hollywood film with a hero and a villain. You could identify with the hero because you got to know who he was, what he dreamed of, and what he feared. The villain was pure evil, and all you got to know about him was what he wanted: Power, revenge, money. But why he wanted that . . . The villain is always an obstacle, and that's why you have a happy ending if the hero kills him. The villain doesn't have any motives, dreams, or uncertainties—he's not actually human. This is the role that fundamentalism is often assigned in the big Western media: They hate us, and we have to get rid of them. And how exactly are we going to do that? Watch *Inside the Middle East* tonight, here on CNN.

Western reporting of Al-Qaida in the aftermath of 9/11 was one-sided, and in retrospect it's easy to figure out why. Who could have explained the villain's motives? Palestinian and Algerian terrorists had, for example, always explained their massacres to the Western public; we even know that some Palestinians tried to commit their hijacks and attacks just before the evening news in America to make sure they hit the headlines. These terrorist organizations also had Western sympathizers and a "political wing" to explain their demands in the media, clear up misunderstandings, and participate in talks.

But Bin Laden recorded his video messages in Arabic, used examples from Islamic history that would be incomprehensible to Westerners, and peppered his speeches with clichés about "Zionist crusaders." Al-Qaida had no political wing, and in any case we probably wouldn't have allowed it to speak up in the climate of anger and fear after September 11. As well, following the passage of anti-terrorism legislation, Al-Qaida sympathizers in most Western countries were immediately locked up.

It was quite logical: You're hardly going to give terrorists a free podium. The consequences were that Al-Qaida couldn't respond to Western public opinion, and Bin Laden was almost exclusively explained and analyzed by his opponents—Western and Israeli analysts, and anti-fundamentalist Arabs and Muslims. These directed their attentions to two things: Bin Laden as an Islamic variant of Hitler, and Bin Laden as the kind of extremist who says, like some animal rights activists and anti abortion campaigners, "My truth is the only truth, and I'm right to lay it down with violence."

But Bin Laden's story had a third dimension, and this hardly made the Western media. Western governments had been supporting the most important Arab dictatorships—namely, Saudi Arabia, the Gulf states, Egypt, Jordan, Tunisia, and Algeria—with money, weapons, and intelligence for decades. Bin Laden pointed out this interference in practically every video, and his message could be summarized in two words: Sod off.

There was also a longer version, and it went something like this: Muslims are poor and weak because they are repressed and exploited by dictators. You Westerners support the dictators. If we attack you, we'll drive a wedge between you and the dictators. In any case, we'll draw the attention of ordinary Muslims to the support that their repressors are getting from the West. Then the dictators will fall, and we will be able to reconstruct our territories.

Prominent Westerners often labeled the 9/11 attacks as "a direct assault on Western civilization." But whoever looks at Bin Laden's story will see that he presents his program as one of self-defense. The West—more particularly, America—

might have received a thrashing, but Al-Qaida's guns are directed at the Saudi royal family, the regime in Cairo, and other Arab dictators. According to Bin Laden, the Islamic world is involved in a civil war, America is supporting his opposition in this war, and that's why he hit America. Al-Qaida is not out to rule New York or London, at least not primarily. Mecca is the main prize for him.

This part of Bin Laden's message has remained, for the most part, out of the Western news stream, meaning that very few Westerners know about their enemy's motives. There has been virtually no debate in the West about its support of dictators, and leading figures continued calling on Muslims in the Islamic world to enter into a "discussion about their faith." But a Muslim who starts a debate about the interpretation of Islam in a key country such as Egypt or Saudi Arabia goes straight to prison because talking about faith is also talking about politics. In prison, that Muslim will be tortured by whomever the CIA trained for that purpose.

***

Now, after the event, I can say more precisely what I would have liked to have done differently. For while Al-Qaida was represented with bias, there was another group that remained almost invisible in the Western media in the aftermath of 9/11: The nonviolent faction of political Islam—those Muslims who say they want to express and promote their conservative or fundamentalist interpretations of Islam without violence. These nonviolent fundamentalists were a blind spot for the West, and a very large one. Not only could no one say how many of them there were, we didn't know what they really were, or what their agenda was.

Just as is the case with communists, Zionists, or Catholics, there are underlying conflicts, a wide scale of opinions and interpretations, and enormous differences between Islamic fundamentalists. The difference is that Islamic fundamentalists aren't free to speak openly. Their books are banned, their websites are shut down, and their leaders are tried or murdered. There's no International League of Fundamentalists or any arenas such as the ones that the Vatican and the Zionist World Congress have in which to deliver resolutions or formulate binding conclusions. Whom should I speak to, to find out what the nonviolent fundamentalists really want?

If you interview a leader in the West, you can figure out what his followers think. If the leader subsequently contradicts himself or deviates from his previous line, he's called to account. For instance, how can he get away with telling the media that September 11 was punishment for American interference in the region, if he said at last month's party congress that September 11 was an attack on humanity? If a leader tries this on, he either has to defend himself or resign. That's how power works in a democracy, and that's how, after a few interviews with the leaders, you can get a reasonable insight into the opinions of the groups represented by them. But in a dictatorship, the leadership group represent only themselves.

Nowhere was the problem so acute as with the semi-underground Muslim Brotherhood. This is the largest fundamentalist movement in the world, with branches in every Muslim country. They are not bearded adventurers who excitedly threaten the West in grainy videos or kill kidnap victims; they are doctors, engineers, scientists, and lawyers. They say that they are nonviolent; but, in the past, the brothers have used violence, and factions have spawned Hamas, the Algerian GIA, and Al-Qaida. Muslim Brothers counter that European social democrats aren't outlawed when extreme leftist splinter groups commit attacks; on the other hand, leading figures within the Brotherhood frequently express undemocratic or anti-Semitic sentiments. These are often later withdrawn, denied, or modified, and then these remarks are denied or modified, so the movement's real agenda remains opaque.

What can you do? In retrospect, I think the best way would have been for correspondents to admit their ignorance. I and my colleagues could have said something like, "It's impossible to guess what the nonviolent branch of 'political Islam' is really planning, and I've only been able to speak to a few dozen of them properly. But they seem like decent people; they all say that they want to realize their ideals without using violence, through their local training college, hospital, or law clinic. Perhaps all of these nonviolent fundamentalists were taking me for a ride, but I don't think these people lay awake in bed at night wondering how to destroy the West. They'd be more likely to be lying awake wondering how to prevent the West from destroying them. What we in the West see as 'development aid' and 'consciousness-raising,' they see as a foreign power using donor darlings and political pressure behind the scenes to try to change them, their beliefs, their male-female social relationships, and the relationship between gays and straights, and between old and young. Supporters of political Islam feel threatened by this kind of interference," I'd end. "They want to shape their own futures, but that doesn't make them instant terrorists."

Perhaps we correspondents should have tried to make the "nonviolent fundamentalists" more visible in this manner, but it was always going to be a tough sell. We just didn't know what we were looking at.

Here is one final example of how this fed through to the reporting. After 9/11, the Egyptian regime ran a number of show trials of members of the Muslim Brotherhood. A show trial is by definition public, so I found myself in a military court on the road that leads to the Suez Canal, next to a cage containing seventy-eight men.

It was like a zoo, only the men were behind the bars, while pigeons flew in and out of the holes in the roof, cooing and crapping. Outside, billboards lauded the greatness of the Egyptian fighting forces; inside was chaos, women holding up babies, and inconsolable teenagers who stood on tiptoes to wave or to push food through the bars. The men had already spent months without any contact with the outside world, and their families knew that after they'd been sent down they'd see them for precisely three minutes every six months. I copied this down in my notebook, since it was a "telling piece of information"—three minutes every six months.

It was the day that the military judge would assess the evidence against the men, who stood accused of having orchestrated an "attempted coup." The prosecutor presented his first piece of evidence, at which point the public tribune chanted, "Reject! Reject!" The judge looked at the baseball bat in question—the only weapon seized in the case—handed it to an agent, and said, "I reject this." Those present applauded the ruling that this evidence did not count. "*Allahu akbar*," came from inside the cage, and one suspect even cried out, "Judge! I'm fifty-five. I'm much too old for a coup. I'm a granddad!" Grins all round from the lawyers and some of the suspects. Second piece of evidence: Books that anyone could buy on any street corner, and cardboard boxes with magazines about technology and aeronautical engineering. The judge said loudly, "I reject these." Cue more cheering.

Then came the lawyer for the defense, and he proved without much difficulty that the "crown witness" was a different person from whom he said he was, and that the police had raided a different house than they said. His final piece was a tape recording on which the suspects were supposed to have been discussing their revolutionary plans. It played only static. For a while, the mood in the barracks was almost jovial. What was the regime up to?

The answer came a couple of months later, when the judge sentenced everyone to years of forced labor. The suspects had no right to appeal, and the presiding "officer" was, of course, not a judge. The sentence he handed down had been decided in advance, just like the results of an Arab election.

That's how the show trials went. If human rights activists or other donor darlings had been in that cage, Western media and politicians would have screamed blue murder. But the defendants were "fundamentalists"—they were lumped together with Al-Qaida, and so the regime could do with them as it wished. In fact, because forced labor in the Egyptian heat is a death sentence for older people, the verdict was tantamount to authorizing dozens of murders. In Egypt alone, tens of thousands of people have been thrown into prison after similar show trials, and no one has said a thing. In the meantime, the Egyptian regime receives 2 billion dollars' worth of weapons and cash from the United States each year.

If I had to sum up the Arab world by using one image, it would be that show trial: Regimes stamping out opposition—more often than not on the sly—under the cover of arguing that they are terrorists. The West stands by, looks on and, when necessary, offers a helping hand. That's why you can't decide whether the opposition is the Islamic variant of fascism or the Islamic variant of Christian democracy.

The truth is missing in dictatorships; that's what makes the system so enduring. But there was more that made the Middle East opaque, and for that I had to go to Lebanon and the Holy Land.

PART II

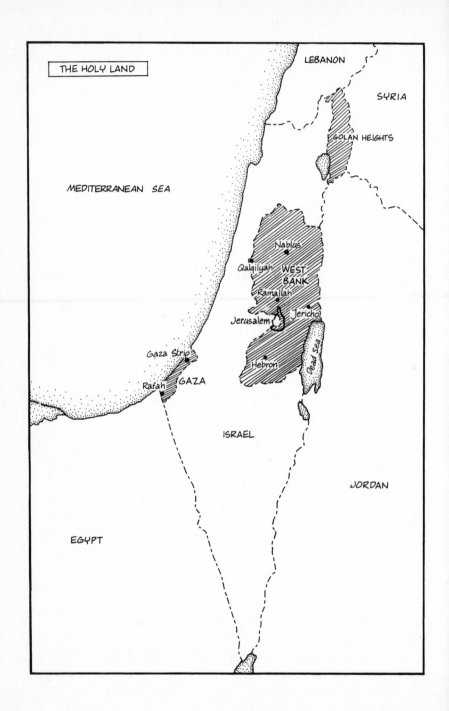

THE HOLY LAND

LEBANON

SYRIA

GOLAN HEIGHTS

MEDITERRANEAN SEA

Nablus

Qalqilyah WEST
BANK

Ramallah

Jerusalem · Jericho

Dead Sea

Gaza Strip

Rafah GAZA

Hebron

ISRAEL

JORDAN

EGYPT

Chapter Seven

A New World

In a book you can tell the important stories one after another, but in life they often overlap. For this reason, I have to take a step backwards in time, to under a year before the 9/11 attacks radically transformed my job as correspondent.

I transferred to another Dutch broadsheet, the *NRC Handelsblad,* where I could focus more on background pieces. I also went to work for the *NOS Journaal* television news program, where I'd be able to study the medium of television from the inside. And I decided to move—I'd had enough of the pollution and third world chaos of Cairo, and a couple of unpleasant things had happened to me.

I'd gotten into an Egyptian prison through the Dutch acquaintance of an inmate, and had come out feeling disgusted. After enduring the spectacle, in the boiling heat, of twenty men being confined in a cell measuring fifteen square meters, their feet having become deformed by enforced standing, and infections and sores caused by the toilet being in the cell . . . Suddenly, I'd had enough of the cruelty with which some Egyptians treated their fellow men. I almost exploded at a taxi driver when he refused to get out of the way of a blaring ambulance, and a few weeks later at the zoo I knew that I wanted a trial separation from Cairo. It was full of unhealthy animals in rusty cages, rancid shrubbery, and rubbish everywhere. Worst of all were some of the visitors, screaming hysterically until one of the monkeys had a heart-wrenching panic attack, bombarding the elephants with fruit and stones, and feeding plastic to the giraffes. I was at the zoo with a Dutch girlfriend, and the kids kept throwing stones at us, too—apparently, we fell into the same category as the animals. As these things go, the kids egged each other on, until one of them dared to run up to us and say: "*Fuckyouwoman!*" That's when the lights went out for me; when they came back on, the kid was lying on the ground. Bystanders hurried over to us and I began to apologize, but everyone reacted with complete understanding, and the boy offered his excuses. I'd always kept my cool in the past when faced with little bastards like these, but I was never shown so much respect as when I crossed the line with violence. *I have to get away from here*, I decided, there and then.

I looked at a map and thought, *What place is more logical to go to than Lebanon?* In the clichéd terms of the travel guides, it was the Switzerland of the Middle East, with snow-topped mountains, and an educated and cosmopolitan population. To Lebanon, then . . . but I'd barely arrived when there were more changes. The peace process between

Israel and Palestine ran aground in a new and violent conflict—what came to be known as the second intifadah. My colleagues in Tel Aviv and Jerusalem had previously covered both Israel and Palestine; but when the violence escalated, I was called up.

So as well as covering the Arab world, I went to do another Big Story, and what a story it was. After the September 11 attacks, the Arab world had certainly become "closer" for the Europeans; however, as a diplomat explained, "Arabs and Palestinians are foreign policy; Israel is domestic news."

I spoke to that diplomat during my first reception at the Dutch embassy in Tel Aviv. In Cairo and Beirut, I'd been to four of these receptions; each time, whenever the Dutch national anthem was played, everyone had stood around sniggering in a typically Dutch way. In Tel Aviv, the same thing happened; but then the Israeli anthem was put on, and many of those present suddenly sang along heartily. This was new—sober Dutch people singing a national anthem with tears in their eyes, and a Dutch embassy playing the anthem of its host country. A while later, one of the guests told me that he sold apartments in Tel Aviv to Dutch Jews who no longer found Amsterdam safe because of its Moroccan youth gangs. Another said that he sold Amsterdam apartments to Dutch Jews who no longer found Tel Aviv safe because of the Palestinian attacks.

Reactions from the Netherlands also showed that my countrymen invested much more emotional capital in Israel and Palestine than in the Arab world. I'd received a few letters in response to my articles about the Arab world, but not many. On one occasion, someone with an Arabic last name had criticized the skewed image of his home region, and an Arabic embassy had once tried to explain away a human rights violation. Apart from that, it was pretty quiet; if I did receive letters, they were farcical. I'd recently trekked through the Sinai desert like the Israelites had in the Bible— in my case, though, for the travel supplement. They'd roamed around for years and I'd done so just for three days, but I hadn't been able to wash any more than they had. I'd commented on this, at which a Bible-thumping pensmith had written in to inform me that the people of Israel cannot have stunk because it said in the Bible that they were very clean. I framed this kind of letter on the wall, just as I'd laughed off terse subscription cancellations: "You're telling me things I don't want to know! Enough of that paper of yours!"

When it came to Israel and Palestine, the laughter soon stopped. After just a few articles and cross-talks, an unstoppable flood came my way—faxes with crucifixes, threats, and accusations. If I made a factual error about the Arab world, the news floor would occasionally receive a letter saying, "Your correspondent has made a factual error." If I made a factual error about Israel, five letters would arrive saying, "Your correspondent is anti-Semitic." One time, I picked up the telephone and heard, "You're going to die." Even my colleague in Tel Aviv was attacked by a Dutch-speaking Israeli: "You're in for it if that Luyendijk carries on writing those articles."

It was a new world, and not just because my readers and viewers were emotionally involved. I'd occasionally used the words "media war" in an article, but it wasn't until I was covering Israel and Palestine that I came to understand what they stood for. In a media war, everything is different, as became clear from my first trip.

The second intifadah had been going on for a few weeks by then. In the beginning, the casualties were mainly Palestinian, but then a crowd in Ramallah lynched two Israeli reservists in front of various camera teams who happened to be in the city. That same evening, Israel bombarded Palestinian cities for the first time since 1967; that was the signal for the world's press to converge on the Holy Land, and for the *NRC* newspaper and the NOS broadcasting channel to enlist me.

Wide-eyed, I walked around the astonishingly quickly erected, yet superbly equipped press center in the five-star Isrotel in the Jewish part of Jerusalem. I'd seen Hezbollah and Arab dictatorship press centers, but this was of a different order. As I hesitated over free coffee, tea in eight different flavors, three types of fruit juice, and piles of bread-roll sandwiches, young Israeli men and women walked round in olive-green army uniforms handing out sheets of great quotes. In efficient, friendly, and fluent English, they told us about the forthcoming press conference and the briefing later that day to be given by a defense specialist.

It was so professional: Pictures of the lynching, route descriptions to the cemetery where the reservists were buried . . . The world's media were given everything they needed with practiced skill, and more: Rights-free archive material of Israeli soldiers giving first aid to Palestinians; the phone numbers of spokesmen who could explain the government's perspective in any major language and in the required number of words; dossiers full of information; print-outs of websites, and piles of leaflets entitled "Terror or occupation—which came first?"

I came across countless journalists who seemed to find this totally normal as they paced up and down across the rugs, discussing the finer details of what they would produce for their newsroom back home, and when and how, with their mobiles clamped to their ears. Jerusalem Capital Studios, which had the satellite connection that correspondents used for their cross-talks with the news programs, was situated next to the Isrotel. This was handy, since many a reporter was expected to give an account of events that same evening, even though he or she had barely set foot upon Israeli, let alone Palestinian, soil.

What kind of world was this? The intifadah escalated, I shuttled between Lebanon and the Holy Land, and with every trip my astonishment grew. A complete alphabet of "optimistic stories" had been cooked up for the correspondents: Jewish, Christian, and Islamic children together in one school; olive branches from Israelis and Palestinians; joint musical performances. You only had to telephone the Palestinian or Israeli organizers of these hopeful projects . . . and the great quotes, checkable information, and striking visual details would be served to you on a plate.

The Israeli government press office called me up. "We've got an exclusive for you: A Dutch-speaking Jewish woman who has voluntarily joined the army because she realizes that Israel is in danger; an English-speaking terrorism expert who can explain what that danger consists of; and a settler whose son was killed in one of the attacks." An American correspondent told me that her TV station only flew in reporters for a couple of weeks. "They've got to score, score, score. When someone comes up with a ready-made script, they jump at it." Next time I saw a settler crying his eyes out on television, I couldn't stop myself from wondering how many camera crews he'd already taken to his son's grave. And how is something like that set up? "You're speaking to the government press office. Our condolences for the loss of your child. I've got three journalists here, and it's your patriotic duty to talk to them about your grief?"

I visited a six-story block of flats in Gaza that had just been bombed by Israel. I spoke to neighbors and surviving relatives, and looked for clean-cut illustrations of clichés like despair and bewilderment. A woman told me that the thought that she had to get the washing machine repaired was still going round in her mind. "But then I realized that it lay underneath the rubble. Just like my husband." Bingo, great quote, and as I went off I saw someone laying brand-new babies' clothes under the debris, for the camera crews who were on their way.

Every few days I experienced something like this, and the most remarkable thing was the openness with which media manipulation was discussed in Israel. After enduring an attack that caused a high civilian death toll, the Israeli government would wait a standard twenty-four hours before retaliating. The world's press was given time to pause and reflect on Israeli suffering because, as soon as Israel took revenge, that would dominate the headlines. The Hassadah hospital in Jerusalem allowed camera crews to visit victims of terrorism so they could "show as much blood, pain and tears as possible," to use the words of an Israeli spokesperson. After one exceptionally large Palestinian attack, the bodies of the victims weren't removed immediately because the prime minister wanted to record his statement in front of a backdrop of eighteen body bags and a burned-out bus. Other examples of the candor with which Israelis discussed influencing the media included an Israeli government minister heartily complimenting a camera crew who had been clever enough to film a few Palestinians cheering after the September 11 attacks—shot in close-up, it looked like there were quite a lot of them, and the clip was often replayed on American TV; the Israeli government press office proudly announcing that it had forced CNN to make a series about the victims of terrorism to make good for having interviewed the relatives of the perpetrator of an attack; and a Jewish–American businessman bragging to the Israeli media that he'd managed to get rid of the critical correspondent of the *Miami Herald* by threatening to withdraw advertisements from it.

***

Before I became a correspondent, I saw a journalist as a kind of a fly on the wall, an invisible microphone recording events, like the football commentators who sit somewhere in the stadium following the score, unseen by the players. But while football might be war, war is not football—not where Israel and Palestine are concerned. The media were continually manipulated and influenced by the parties concerned.

It was a new world, and fellow journalists explained to me what lay behind it. I'd thought that a media war was a war with a lot of media attention, but it went further than that. Compare the second intifadah with the border conflict being fought at the same time between Ethiopia and Eritrea, colleagues said. That was a classic war: Two parties fight each other with all the military might they have; the strongest wins; and the media report on that. But the conflict between Israel and Palestine is orchestrated differently. If they both threw everything they had into it, the case would be instantly settled. Israel rules supreme with its nuclear weapons, smart bombs, hyper-advanced tanks, fighter jets, helicopters, battleships, surveillance satellites, and submarines. Within twenty-four hours, it could drive off the Palestinians and, if it wanted to, all of its neighbors, too. This is something that some Israeli media and politicians regularly advocate. But it won't happen, and you can't separate that from the enormous media attention devoted to this area and the involvement of public opinion worldwide. And this public opinion is largely formed by what people see in the media.

Hello, everybody! As an Israeli PR manager said, "It's not about what happens, but how it is presented on CNN." In the Holy Land, newspaper pages and television screens weren't just windows on the conflict—they were also a stage on which the conflict was being fought.

Chapter Eight

The Law of the Scissors

My next stop was Ramallah, and I was scared. A Palestinian crowd had lynched two Israeli reservists, leading to the first Israeli bombing of Palestinian cities since 1967. The images I'd seen on every channel! First, cheering Palestinians hold up part of an Israeli corpse, and then the shelling starts— people walk happily along the street, they look up in surprise, there's an enormous bang and clouds of smoke, and people run in all directions.

But when I arrived in Ramallah, it was all business as usual. The market had been set up, taxis tooted at customers and, yes, if you turn right at the end of the street and right again at the hoarding advertising Persil washing powder, you'll find the one police station that Israel has meticulously bombed . . . You know what, I'll come along with you. That was the atmosphere the day after the lynching and the bombing—but if I switched on Arab or Western stations, reporters were excitedly talking about "tension on the streets of Ramallah," "boiling rage," and "enormous concern," followed by footage of the lynching and the bombing.

It was in Ramallah that I first noticed how television determines your view of reality: You don't know what you are *not* being shown, and what you are shown makes a much larger impression than newspaper articles or radio programs. A colleague of mine neatly summed it up: Words target your mind; images hit you in the gut. Once in a cross-talk with the television news team, I related how young girls in Gaza stopped menstruating after the Israeli bombings. Puberty was reversed by stress. I knew about this because I'd just written two big stories about the psychological effects of Israeli violence on Palestinian schoolchildren. They'd been given prominent spots in the *NRC*; but, in the days following the news broadcast, various editors called up to ask whether I couldn't write a story about the psychological effects of Israeli violence on Palestinian schoolchildren. Didn't you read my articles, I asked. And often the answer was, "Well, now that you mention it . . . ."

Television was king in the media war being played out in the Holy Land, but it turned out to have its weak points. Before I'd seen television crews at work, I'd always watched the news with a fairly trusting attitude. I'd had no idea what was out of shot when a Palestinian woman stood in front of the ruins of her bombarded house, raised her hands to the heavens, and cried: "My children!" The emotion might well be authentic, but when I saw a shot like that being filmed in Gaza, I realized that viewers were watching something other than a private emotional outburst. The woman was crying out "My children!" while, two feet away from her, a muscular bloke was trying to angle his camera so that the raised hands didn't get in the way of the close-up of her face. There was a mike dangling two feet above the crying woman's head, and around her you'd have an interviewer, his interpreter, and often a gathering—camera teams draw people like bread draws ducks. How had the team found this woman? Of course, it could be that the cameraman had spotted her and taken the shot without her permission. But it was more likely that an interviewer had chosen one woman from a small group; that there'd been a bit of chat while the light was being measured; that she'd been positioned so the sun didn't produce any backlighting, and the rubble was visible but not dominating; that the neighborhood rascals had been persuaded to be quiet; and that, after a gesture from the soundman, the interviewer had asked, via the interpreter, "What happened to your children?"

At university I had memorized stuff about the medium being the message—the theory that form determines content in television—but the extent to which circumstances effect what you do or don't get to show on the box was something I didn't really get until I'd been to Lebanon to film there myself.

The reportage was supposed to be about Palestinian reactions to former general Ariel Sharon's comeback in Israeli politics. Sharon had been the brains behind the Israeli invasion of Lebanon, twenty years previously, when Israeli troops were in control of the Palestinian refugee camps of Sabra and Shatila, and a Lebanese Christian militia had slaughtered twelve hundred people. The militia had been armed, trained, and bankrolled by Israel, and had been allowed to do its thing for two days and two nights, lit by Israeli flares. The blood-bath had made Sabra and Shatila world famous and had cost Sharon his place in politics, but he was back. In the words of a Palestinian ice cream salesman: "In former Yugoslavia, war criminals get locked up; in Israel, they get made prime minister."

The Hilversum studios sent over an NOS colleague to show me the ropes. We hired a local camera team, pro-ceeded to the camps, and that's when I made a mistake I'm still ashamed of. Talking with camp inhabitants, I stumbled across some "inconvenient data," as anthropologists call it—information that doesn't fit with your story. Palestinians told me that the so-called War against the Camps a few years later had been much worse than the infamous refugee-camp bloodbath. "That was terrible," they said, "but it only lasted two days." The war for control over the camps years later, on the other hand, had lasted months: They talked about starva-tion, and described nauseating acts of brutality perpetrated by Syrians and the Amal Shiite militia (*amal* means "hope" in Arabic).

Then I slipped up as a journalist. I should have changed the angle of the story, or at least worked this part of it into the reportage. But I'd come to do a story about Sharon's come-back, and I simply missed the double standards that kept indirect Israeli responsibility for twelve hundred deaths in the news for twenty years, while a much larger massacre by Syrians or Lebanese was forgotten.

We carried on looking for people who'd lost family mem-bers in the right bloodbath. The soundman came up with a chap whose two nephews had been murdered. Was that enough? After an awkward conversation, we discovered that he hadn't been there during the massacre. A direct witness would be much better, but how could we say that politely? We encountered Soha, a young women in her mid-twenties. She'd gone to look at the Israeli soldiers at the time: "Everyone said the Jews had horns, and I wanted to see that." The militia missed Soha while she was out of the camp, but her family had less luck. Mobile telephones off, camera, action! And Soha began to cry. She told the story through her tears, then the camera was switched off and she recovered herself. "Shall I act out how I hid from the militia?" She pulled a childish face and mimed peering out from behind an imaginary wall. "That's what I did for French television."

Hello, everybody! That's why the cameraman had chatted so casually with Soha—he knew her from previous recordings. We carried on our search and crossed our fingers for some good interviews. Then we had to go to the editing suite, and that's where the difference between television and the newspapers really became clear. I also wrote an article for the *NRC* about the Palestinian refugees in Sabra and Shatila. It began like this:

> Meryam Abdelhadi still has the heavy radio her father carried with him when he fled their home in what is now northern Israel, along with his family of eleven. In 1948, after the creation of Israel, a war broke out and rumors of massacres perpetrated by Jewish soldiers did the rounds. "We thought it would only be for a few days," Abdelhadi told me in her house in Shatila. "We took the radio and a battery so we'd know when we could go back. But the Jews didn't let us go back." More than fifty years later, mother of eight, Abdelhadi, is still waiting to return.[9]

Meryam Abdelhadi was the most appealing case in the camp, and that old radio provided a good opening. It was an everyday example which illustrated that Palestinians never realized what was hanging over their heads; holding onto that radio symbolized their perseverance.

But Abdelhadi didn't make the television news. Her radio was at a friend's house, and he wasn't home. She wanted to tell the story of her murdered sisters, but she kept digressing and lost herself in details. There was a buzzing sound from the shop downstairs, and her house was much too dark for our equipment. Once she understood that we could only film her if we were able to move the cupboard, the chairs, the television, and the sofa, she politely asked us to find someone else.

There went our piece for the TV news. Her story, and the phone number of the friend who had the radio, were enough for me to be able to write an article—I could check the facts beforehand—but television has to show the radio in question. In the paper, I could use the great quote from the ice cream seller about the difference between Yugoslav and Israeli war criminals; but for the TV news he'd have to say it on camera, and he was nowhere to be found.

Abdelhadi's chaotic way of talking was not a problem for the *NRC* because I could cut, summarize, and extract things from what she had said. I was able to put together a story with words, and my word processor allowed me to take it in any direction. With television montage, though, you have to make do with what you've got on film. After all, you tell the story with images—so it's quite logical that if you don't have an image, you don't have a story. "Can't I explain it in words then, if we don't have the images?" I asked my colleague (the one showing me the ropes). But that was terribly difficult on television because of the Law of the Scissors.

My colleague had to explain it to me, because I'd only learned to analyze texts, never images, at secondary school. The Law of the Scissors describes the effect that images have on people. Images take precedence over sound, so if the voice-over explains something different from the images, the viewer follows only the images. If you read out, "We are learning more and more about the way Palestinians were ethnically cleansed during the creation of Israel" while showing footage of goals scored by FC Maccabi Tel Aviv, the content of the voice-over won't sink in. "The scissors are open," TV producers say. If you exchange the goals for footage of Palestinians fleeing, the blades of the scissors come closer together. Image and sound support each other. This is television at its best, more powerful than any newspaper article. The problem, of course, is that many things in the world can't be filmed. Leaving the screen blank and reading out the text isn't an option for television, but any image you put "behind" the spoken word will push aside the verbal account.

On television, the Law of the Scissors reduced reality to what was filmable, and the consequences of this were evident when a media battle erupted over suicide bombings. There were two very different stories to tell about the people who committed such attacks. You might say that the lives of those freedom fighters were obviously so devoid of hope that they were prepared to die for their cause; it must be terrible to live under occupation. You might also say that these terrorists clearly hated Israelis more than they loved their own lives; ergo, Palestinians must be terrible people.

The Israeli PR machine propagated the latter explanation,

of course, and was helped enormously by the parents of the suicide bombers. As soon as someone blew himself up, the news agency camera crews raced to the parents' homes, and often they would say how proud they were, and that they would stand behind any other children who did the same.

I visited a family like this: The Abu Kweiks in Gaza. Their twenty-one-year-old son, Arafat, a final-year education student at the Islamic University of Gaza, had charged at some Israeli soldiers, his body packed with explosives. Now the Abu Kweiks were sitting in front of their stinking concrete hovel in the refugee camp called "The Beach," and were being congratulated by their neighbors.

Father Qassam told us that Arafat had even bid him farewell. "I was half asleep. He stuck his head around the corner and said a quick goodbye." He paused. "If I'd have known, I'd have given him a hug." A neighbor came past, and Qassam said, "My son is not dead; martyrs go straight to heaven and live on there. May my other sons become martyrs, too, and may I join them. Death to all Jews!" He related that he was going to donate the ten thousand dollars that Saddam Hussein gave to every "martyr's" family to the mosque. "If my son had wanted money he'd have become a collaborator," he told everybody. "My son is a hero and he is in heaven." A Hamas functionary dropped off the poster of Mohammed that was being circulated. The father politely accepted it; one minute you've got a son; the next, a martyr. Dates were passed around, Coca-Cola, copies of Arafat's farewell letter and tea—with sugar, because this death was not bitter.

After recounting how creative, pious, and studious his son was, Qassam gave me a tour of the ruins he called his home. Arafat's brother Yasser came with us. He was now the oldest son of the household, a big responsibility in such a large family. "I want to show you something," he whispered to me, "but not in my father's presence." He went towards his own room; his father made to follow him, but Yasser gestured "no." I hadn't seen a Palestinian son do this before. Yasser closed the door firmly, picked up a plastic bin bag, and began to take some clothes out of it. "I got these from Hamas," he explained. They were the clothes that Arafat had worn for the attack. A terrible stench filled the room. Yasser fingered the myriad bullet holes in the trousers. The top part of the jacket was missing, because Arafat's body had been ripped apart by a grenade before he'd even been able to get close to the Israeli soldiers. "I've got no idea what to do with these," Yasser whispered. "It was Arafat's own decision." We stood there numbly, and I stared at his posters of an Egyptian football team and a Lebanese singer. Yasser put the bag away, and we were about to leave when I asked him why his father couldn't come with us. Yasser blinked. "My father is only just holding it together. If he saw these clothes, the bullet holes and that torn jacket . . . it would kill him."

Hello, everybody! From the Internet, I got the name of one of the few psychiatrists in Gaza, the internationally renowned human rights activist, Iyad Serraj. He'd just been beaten up by guerrillas from the Palestinian authority because he'd criticized the Leader, but he still wanted to see me.

"I'm often in touch with the Voo," he said over the phone. What? Oh, the VU, the Vrije Universiteit (Free University) in Amsterdam! According to Serraj, Arafat's parents were demonstrating a classic reaction to trauma: Denial. "Of course they are saying they're happy. It's a way of delaying mourning, and that's normal, but once the cameras have gone, the anger and depression hit. Then they come here—on occasion, because psychiatric problems are taboo." With a skillfulness that betrayed the fact he'd told this story a few times already, Serraj told me that Hamas records a farewell video as soon as anyone offers themselves up as a suicide bomber, and then they're not allowed to tell anyone about it. "Months can go by before Hamas calls up the volunteer," Serraj said. "But the video is a kind of contract that it is hard to go back on. Why does Hamas put volunteers under so much pressure? Why can't they talk to anyone about it? If their parents were really happy about it, wouldn't they encourage such an act?"

I tried to check up on Serraj's story. Psychiatric problems amongst Palestinians did indeed appear to be taboo: No figures were kept, and there was almost no support available. I visited a few families who'd lost someone in the preceding months. One father showed me the home renovations he'd had done with Saddam Hussein's martyrs' payout; another recounted how months went by before Hamas came to tell them that their son had blown himself up. Nobody seemed delighted or proud, and one mother referred to her son's suicide as, "the umpteenth disaster in my life."

Serraj seemed to have a point, and he was more than happy to appear on TV. Sometimes I saw him on Western or Arabic channels, but his story turned out to be incommensurably less powerful than the images of proud and delighted Palestinian parents. Ideally, you wouldn't have Serraj but the depressed parents or, better still, Arafat Abu Kweik's brother saying what it was really like. But they only told their stories when the camera was turned off. And, of course, if there were no images, there was no story.

***

Making television is a time-consuming exercise, and I wasn't very good at it. I also felt intensely constrained because circumstances governed what I could or couldn't show. Palestinians were clearly not used to television: They gave five-minute answers to every question, while the entire piece-to-air had a limit of three minutes and twelve seconds. "We can cut it, though, can't we?" I asked the first time. But that would make the image jump, and this is so distracting that you lose the viewer's attention. Often, the Palestinians only dared to talk about interesting things—the corruption within their authorities, for example—once the cameras were turned off. I could overcome this problem by mentioning it myself (we call it a *stand-upper* in the jargon; but I could only do this once, and even then it had less impact than if it had come out of a Palestinian's mouth—and what could you do if you wanted to bring up three more cases that people would only talk about off the record? No pictures, no story.

It was enough to drive you mad, and it became even clearer why Western correspondents fell back on their fixers. These correspondents would make a day trip to Palestine from their home base in Israel and be met by a fixer who had a list ready for them: "I've got a collaborator who is on death row, a mother whose child was shot dead for throwing stones, a woman who had a miscarriage at a checkpoint, a farmer who has lost his land, a tortured detainee, four sisters who opened up a sewing factory after their home was destroyed . . ."

Fixers get at least a hundred dollars a day, and it's likely that the people on their lists get a share of this. In which case, who could guarantee that they wouldn't just say the things that had gone down so well with the previous Western camera crews? Most of the fixers worked for the Palestinian

Authority in their daily lives, with the consequence that they weren't available to them just when they were needed the most. That's like the official heads of all the important Dutch ministries moonlighting for CNN right after a local disaster.

When I first found out about fixers, I found it scandalous. But after I'd tried making television a few times myself, my shock waned. With television you had to adapt as best you could to the circumstances as they were, if only because the warring parties were doing that, too. Those manipulating the media knew about the Law of the Scissors, and realized that I was in their hands as long as I only had footage that made them look good.

Manipulation of this kind became easier the greater the time pressure on us, which I experienced firsthand when I had to go to Ramallah again. Israel had killed the leader of a Palestinian splinter group; members of that group had taken revenge by murdering an Israeli minister; Israel had ordered the murderers be given up, which the then-leader, Arafat, had refused to do; and so Israeli tanks had besieged Arafat's headquarters. Film crews could still get in, and Arafat gave a statement by candlelight that he wouldn't yield under pressure and would leave as a "martyr" if necessary—powerful images shown endlessly by Arabic broadcasters.

The stalemate lasted until Israel and Arafat reached a complicated compromise in which the leaders of the splinter group would be imprisoned but in a Palestinian jail, under British supervision. The tanks withdrew, and Palestinian spokespersons crowed about their victory. "The humiliating siege is over and Arafat is a national hero." This became the stuff of news agency reports, to which the opposition in Israel exclaimed: "Look how stupid our government is—Arafat's been made a national hero."

These reactions became news agency reports, too, just like Arafat's victory tour through Ramallah that morning, with triumphant Palestinians on the roadsides and a class of children who sang: "We support you with our blood and our souls, dear Arafat." CNN and the BBC took up these images, complete with the victorious statements given by the Palestinian spokespersons. My editors in Hilversum had seen this and put together a storyline: Siege broken—survival artist Arafat pulls it off again. It looked like a straightforward story, and I hurried to Ramallah. The plan was to get a few quotes from ordinary Palestinians, link everything together in a piece-to-camera, and then shoot back to the studio in West Jerusalem for the montage.

But nobody in Ramallah would talk to the camera, I didn't see any revelry or spontaneous demonstrations, and the atmosphere was subdued. I made a few calls, dropped in on my usual juice, newspaper, and shish-kebab people, and everything I heard suggested that ordinary Ramallah residents were not at all happy or proud. They were disillusioned because they felt that their leader had given into Israeli demands yet again. Arafat's victory tour had been a set-up for the cameras, and the triumphant crowds had been made up of perhaps a hundred Palestinian Authority employees drummed up for the occasion.

As a newspaper journalist, I could cover the other story at such moments, but where would I find the images to tell that different story on television? My report had been booked to screen that evening, and thousands of euros had been spent on the camera crew, on hours in the montage suite, and on the radio link. I was in competition with other reporters, who I could imagine saying, "That Luyendijk can't cope with real work, and now he's saying CNN has got it wrong." In the end, I put together as noncommittal a report as possible, like a politician who lies not by telling falsehoods, but by keeping silent about a crucial part of the truth.

Chapter Nine

"They Are Killing Innocent Jews"

The Holy Land was a new world, and I resolved to be extra cautious and always objective. I knew how strongly different members of the Dutch community empathized with each side, how eager the fighting parties were to manipulate the media, and how vulnerable television in particular was to this.

But was it even possible to be objective? I hadn't worried about it all beforehand, because didn't the second-largest American news channel, Fox News, say, "We report, you decide"? Didn't Al-Jazeera advertise its strategy as "giving both sides of the story"? And didn't my own paper, the *NRC*, promise "a clear separation between fact and opinion"? Wasn't this the essence of quality journalism—to give the facts as they were, and offer both sides of the argument when reporting people's opinions? This was how you presented an objective picture of a conflict, I thought.

But, quite quickly, doubts set in, and they would only grow in the years that followed. It began with my choice of words. In the Arab world, I'd already been exposed to partisan language: Muslims who based their political orientation on their faith were "fundamentalists," whereas, in most Western media reports, an American presidential candidate with the same religious convictions would be labeled "evangelical" or "deeply religious." If that American won the election, almost nobody would say that Christianity was marching forwards; but when Muslims who were inspired in their politics by the Koran came out on top, many a Western commentator would say that Islam was on the march. If an Arab leader clashed with a Western government, he was "anti-Western"; Western governments were never "anti-Arab."

In Cairo I'd collected a few examples, and in the Holy and the list grew rapidly: Hamas is "anti-Israeli"; Jewish s ttlers are not "anti-Palestinian." Palestinians who use viole ce against Israeli citizens are "terrorists"; Israelis who use vic ence against Palestinian citizens are "hawks" or "hardline s." Israeli politicians who seek a peaceful resolution are "do es"; their Palestinian equivalents are "moderates"— impl ing that deep down all Palestinians are fanatics. You could see the double standards more clearly if you turned things around: "Moderate Jew Shimon Peres's anti-Islamic speech has caused great unrest amongst Palestinian doves."

This was how you could be biased, purely by labeling compara ble cases differently for each camp. But in the Holy Land it c dn't stop at this kind of "asymmetrical word use."

In the Arab dictatorships there was usually just one word for everyt ing, which kept things simple. Everyone just calls

Egypt "Egypt," but Israel could also be called "the Zionist entity" or "occupied Palestine." Were the areas in question "occupied," "disputed," or "liberated," or rather the West Bank of the Jordan River, or Judea and Samaria, or the Palestinian territories? Were they Jewish villages, Jewish settlements, or illegal Jewish settlements? Should I talk about Jews, Zionists, or Israelis? Not all Zionists are Jews, not all Jews are Israelis, and not all Israelis are Jewish. Were they Arabs, Palestinians, or Muslims? Not all Arabs are Palestinians, not all Palestinians are Muslim, and not all Muslims are Palestinian.

This was the first problem in the Holy Land: If you wanted to be objective, there were no neutral terms. And you couldn't just list all the terms: "Today in Ramallah, on the occupied or disputed or liberated West Bank of the Jordan River or Samaria, two Palestinians or Muslims or Arab newcomers or terrorists or freedom fighters were killed or slaughtered by Israeli soldiers or Israeli defense forces or Zionist occupying troops . . ."

When I only covered the Arab world and followed the Holy Land through the media, I'd noticed that there was more than just one word for everything. I'd regarded it as a local custom, a good topic for the culture section: Did they argue even about that? But stuck in the middle of it, I realized that that was precisely what they were arguing about. Those words used together made up a viewpoint, and there were so many words because there were so many viewpoints.

There was something else that made the Holy Land a new world—you could work there as a correspondent and be able to observe all the viewpoints. Israel is a democracy, with the complete freedom of expression that goes with that. I didn't speak Hebrew, but you had English-language newspapers, and sometimes Israeli TV programs were subtitled in Arabic—at the end of the day, it was the country's second language. The Palestinians, in turn, lived under a remarkable combination of an indirect Israeli occupation and the semi-dictatorship of the Palestinian Authority. The Authority had ministers, police, and security services, and enjoyed the "limited self-government" of a handful of enclaves. For the Palestinians it was a mixture of two types of repression, which differed per enclave, but there was so much space that most Palestinians did want to talk, certainly if I arrived with sufficient time on my hands and no interpreter.

In this way I was able to pick out different standpoints and compare them, and quite quickly I became embarrassed about the view I'd previously had of the conflict between Israel and the Palestinians, which was that you had supporters of peace and opponents of peace—the most exciting question being who was going to win.

Now I could talk to those "opponents of peace," and not one of them said: "Peace? Are you crazy? That's not what we want." These people dreamed of an end to the conflict, too; they just had different ideas about what was needed to bring it about and whose fault it was that no peace agreement could be reached.

"Peace can only hold out if it's a fair peace," people from Hamas and the Islamic Jihad said. "Fair" would mean that all of the Palestinian refugees could return to the homes they'd fled or been chased from when Israel was founded. Hamas said that Israel wasn't a country but an artificial establishment, a "Zionist entity." The peace process was going to create a powerless reserve; after that, the world would forget the Palestinians, and Israel would discreetly finish them off. This was why Hamas didn't talk about an *amaliyit issalam*, a peace process, but an *amaliyit al-istislam*, a capitulation process.

When Hamas and the Jihad used the words "peace process," they put them between quotation marks. It was a tendency they shared with right-wing Israelis—although the latter didn't appreciate me saying that. According to Likud, the "peace process" was a deadly blunder by the Israelis. Arabs would carry on fighting to destroy the Jewish state. Some at Likud spoke of a *piece process* instead of a peace process: Israel was being given away piece by piece to its enemies.

The peace process's most fierce opponents were probably the fundamentalist Jewish settlers. They believed that God had given them the Promised Land, not just Israel but also Gaza, East Jerusalem, and Judea and Samaria—the West Bank of the Jordan River. These places were not "occupied" but "liberated" and, according to the fundamentalist Jewish settlers, a "peace process" in which even a square meter of land would be transferred to the "Arabic newcomers" would bring not peace but God's wrath. Everything was permissible in order to prevent this—even shooting your own prime minister dead, as the settler Yigar Amir proved in 1995 when he assassinated Yitzak Rabin.

This was the confusing reality behind the simplistic concept of "opponents of peace." The longer I worked on it, the more viewpoints I encountered. The Christian fundamentalists, who numbered at least 30 million in America, believed that the End Time would come at the moment the West Bank was inhabited exclusively by Jews. The atheist wing of the Palestinian–Israeli peace movement strove for a single state for Jews, Muslims, and Christians. Arab nationalists wanted a single Arab Union for Arabic Muslims, Christians, and Jews to cover the region from Iraq to Morocco. The proponents of Greater Israel dreamed of a Jewish state extending from the Tigris in Iraq to the Nile in Egypt. And there was the ultra-orthodox Jews of Shas, the country's third party, who backed out of military service and considered the Holocaust to have been God's punishment for the European Jews' assimilation.

In the Arab world, I'd had to continually guess at the beliefs and opinions of people and of political parties—the blank spots on the map of any dictatorship. In the case of Israel and Palestine, I had at least seven or eight maps, complete with glossaries. I went from guessing to drowning in a sea of information. After an attack, the announcement of a new settlement, or a diplomatic breakthrough, how could you list the reactions of the Jewish, Christian, and Islamic fundamentalists, and of the Israeli government, and of the Palestinian Authority, and of the ultra-orthodox Jews, and of the atheist wing of the peace moment?

It was impossible, and the problem didn't stop there—something I noticed after I'd spent a few evenings surfing the TV channels. The things some broadcasters went big on were not even mentioned on other channels, or were presented completely differently. An attack in Israel might have the headline "Entire country deeply shocked by massacres that killed eight," followed by footage of horrible images, distraught relatives, and the functionally angry spokesperson: "They are killing innocent Jews!" But you could also mention such an incident in the news in brief: "Today, opposition to the Israeli occupation flared up, leading to the deaths of eight Israelis in Tel Aviv." When the Israeli government announced new settlements, it could be done in a business-like fashion with a map of the area showing the new zone in cross-hatching and, at the most, a statement like, "The Palestinian Authority called the expansion a new attack on the peace process." But you could also make it into a big piece with distraught Palestinians whose land had been taken, and a functionally angry Palestinian spokesperson: "How can Israel exchange land for peace if it's going to fill up that land with settlements where only Jews can live?"

Radically different stories could be told about the same events. The Western media had to choose between them, and during my time they opted for the opinions and issues that were relevant to the two parties at the negotiating table. Their priorities dominated the news, and their positions were set against each other's: "According to the Israeli government, the attack proves once again that the Palestinians don't want peace. The Palestinian Authority says the occupation is the problem."

This was how the international media made sense of it all, and with them their viewers, readers, and listeners. But this narrowing of vision brought with it a new problem— that of "objectivity." You could promise to present "just the facts," but which facts? You can show off about getting both sides of the story, but what if there are more than two sides to that story? And then you still have the problem of partisan vocabulary, even if you only put two players under the spotlight. The story of the moment was the derailing of the peace process. Spokespersons from the Palestinian Authority said, "The peace process is about land in exchange for peace. We demand therefore that the 'illegal Jewish settlements' be dismantled and the *occupied* areas be *given back*. How can Israel 'negotiate' over land that it doesn't own?"

Israel spokespersons said, "The peace process is land in exchange for peace. This is what we are negotiating—in exchange for Palestinian concessions, Israel *gives up* part of the *disputed* territories while other 'Jewish settlements' will stay with us. Negotiation always involves give and take." Both positions sounded reasonable; but, depending on whose terms the media used, one or the other party came out of it better.

There were more, many more, problems if you wanted to report on the situation objectively. A media war is also about the sympathy vote. The public generally identify with the weaker power, and so both parties wanted to maneuver themselves into the position of the underdog. They tried to get the blood of their own dead and wounded onto the television as much as possible, while making their opponents look as bad as they could. It was logical but, for the concerned correspondent who wanted to be as objective as he could, it was a new problem. What if one side was able to display its suffering much better than the other? I encountered this right away, on my first trip to the Holy Land, and only later did I realize what I had seen.

It happened during that very first time in the Holy Land, when the Palestinian lynching in Ramallah had sent me rushing over, together with hundreds of colleagues from all over the world. When I arrived I had to go to the sophisticated press center in the Isotel for my press pass. A pre-digested version of the events was waiting for me there: These two people were torn to pieces by rampaging mobs; look what kind of blind hatred Israel has to defend itself

against. Everything—the images, the great quotes, the information dossiers—was tailored to deliver the same message:
"They are killing innocent Jews; the problem is Palestinian
hatred and terrorism."

Next I drove to Ramallah, where there was no press
center, and journalists didn't need to register their presence.
If you called the Ministry of Information no one picked up,
or you finally got an engaged signal after a long wait. The
lynched Israeli soldiers had been reservists. What were two
soldiers from perhaps the best trained army in the world
doing in the center of a city in revolt? You might think that
journalists should take the time to find out. But news happens
too quickly for that; and if a ready-made Palestinian version
of events isn't at hand, the Israeli version will dominate.

The Israeli government was much better equipped than the
Palestinian Authority to fight the media war. When I saw
how the Israeli government handled PR disasters, I understood how that difference fed through to the reporting.

Every now and then, images of Palestinian women and
children who'd been killed by Israeli bullets popped up.
These portrayed the essence of the conflict, according to the
Palestinians: The problem is the occupation, and look at the
brute violence that the Israeli army uses against innocent Palestinian civilians to maintain the occupation.

However, instead of waiting until the storm of bad publicity blew over (as the Palestinian Authority often did), the
Israeli government would launch a counterattack. Prominent
and sincere-looking Israelis immediately would appear on
Western television channels and in opinion pages to declare
that they were ashamed of their country, and that this stain on

the Jewish state had to be investigated in depth. PR officials would express their regret, and emphasize that Israel never meant to kill innocent children, women, or senior citizens—what would the Jewish state gain from that? Often, the same spokespeople would go on to question whether the victims had really died from Israeli bullets . . . This would be investigated most carefully, and that would take some time. Next, the same people would explain how murky such "violent occurrences" in the "disputed territories" were, and how tiny the areas were in which this kind of "tragedy" took place. "Terrorists" deliberately hid in residential areas in the hope that Israel would accidentally kill Palestinian civilians, and so with all this attention to this tragedy we in the media were unintentionally playing into the terrorists' hands.

This was how the Israeli government tried to minimize the damage: leaving the occupation out of it, distancing themselves from the events, isolating them as rare incidents, sowing doubt on the facts, and shifting the blame . . . I had to see this a few times before I understood how poorly the Palestinians had handled the PR fallout from the lynching. Imagine if they'd had a professional PR machine like Israel's, with Palestinian politicians who were popular in the West, human rights activists or writers who'd instantly express their horror and their sympathy for the relatives on CNN or in American opinion pages. Spokespersons could have explained immediately what only came out three days later—that the day before the lynching, the mutilated body of a young Palestinian had been found in a nearby Jewish settlement. This "victim of the Israeli occupation" had just been carried by large crowds to his final resting place (hence the cameras being in Ramallah) when a rumor went round that two Israeli commandos had forced their way into the city for a new "massacre." People were already violently incensed because in previous weeks Israel had killed more than fifty civilians. The spokespersons would have emphasized that nothing could explain away this atrocity—what had the Palestinian Authority to gain from such a lynching? The Palestinians wanted nothing more than what they were entitled to according to the UN and international law: Their own state, and an end to more than three decades of Israeli occupation.

Israeli governments would have handled it this way, but the Palestinian Authority didn't tackle it like this at all. What they did do afterwards was to immediately confiscate all images of the lynching—something that all the Arabic camera teams complied with. An Italian reporter did get his footage out, and was pestered and threatened for weeks by the Authority.

B efore I went to the Holy Land, I had heard of the "Israel Lobby." I understood that the Israeli government could afford the most expensive lawyers and PR agencies in Europe and America, and could count on thousands of extremely well-educated sympathizers, lobbying groups, local branches of Likud and the Labor Party, the World Zionist Organization, and smaller Zionist associations. There were active synagogues and a battery of Christian fundamentalist movements with great influence on the conservative media in America.

Despite this, I hadn't realized how advanced Israeli media policy was. Israeli ambassadors and lobbyists also visited leading editors and producers at television networks, cable news television, and the main daily and weekly newspapers in many Western countries. Pro-Israeli Jewish and Christian

fundamentalist clubs in America invited "good" correspondents and commentators to give lectures, for attractively high
fees. In the same country, former Mossad employees set up
a media center that scoured Palestinian and Arabic press for
anti-Semitic, anti-American, and anti-Western propaganda.
Their reports would turn up verbatim in the press back home
quite regularly—in columns, articles, and parliamentary
questions, often without any mention of the source.

A soft drinks manufacturer once told me he'd carried out
a "gap analysis" in Israel. This was a marketing method to
measure the gap between a product's worth in general and
your brand in particular. Number one: Do you like soft
drinks? Number two: Do you like Pepsi? Whoever answered
yes to the first question and then no to the second would be
sensitive to an advertising campaign. The businessman told
me that the market-research company's client list included
a customer who was mean to remain anonymous. After
insisting, he'd learned who it was: The Israeli PR apparatus
had commissioned its own gap-analysis research among certain defined groups in the West. The questions were, What
do you think of the State of Israel? What do you think of
this particular government? The findings were used for campaigns—for example, to invite specially selected members of
parliament, editors-in-chief, columnists, commentators, trade
unionists, or student leaders on visits to Israel.

That was how it worked, and the investment paid off.
Wafa, the Palestinian news agency—or whatever went by that
name—once announced that Israeli planes were air-dropping
poisoned sweets. They presented no proof, and the Israeli PR
machine went into motion with astonishing speed. Not just
correspondents, but also Dutch members of parliament, columnists, and editors were sent "Black Books" showing that

this kind of propaganda was far from uncommon. There had been official Palestinian "warnings" that the Israeli army was using "depleted uranium, poison gas, and radioactive material"; Palestinian television had broadcast sermons in which Jews were compared to "monkeys and pigs"; and Palestinian schoolbooks contained anti-Israeli passages.

The Israeli government had to have collected this material beforehand and to have waited for a good time to use it. Wafa's statement about poisoned sweets was perfect; it gave journalists, columnists, and MPs a basis from which to mention not just this one instance of incitement, but to extrapolate from it—see how Palestinians are being taught to hate Israel.

It was a professional piece of work, and very effective because the inverse didn't happen. Quite a few Israeli schoolbooks avoid mentioning the fact that Palestinians were living there before the foundation of Israel. Some rabbis want to burn down the Aqsa mosque; Israeli generals have called Palestine "a cancerous growth"; and the ultra-Orthodox Jewish party has pleaded for the "extermination of Arabs." There was enough material for a long-term campaign in which such inciting remarks could be linked to questions such as, "Is this why their soldiers shoot so many Palestinians?" and "Does Israel really want peace?"

But the Palestinian Authority didn't release any Black Books. Correspondents might occasionally report on Israeli propaganda, but such reports remained marginal. Media war is about marketing. The frequency with which you manage to get your message to the target group is just as important as what the message is.

The Israeli government was simply much better at playing the game. During the second intifadah, "violence" alternated with stand offs. A few times, Hamas literally blew up the ceasefire, but other times there were weeks of ceasefire until Israel suddenly liquidated a Palestinian bigwig. A murder like this would be rapidly followed up by a stream of press releases about "increased vigilance" and "extra security measures." It worked quite often; the news mentioned "Israel's fear after liquidation," instead of "Israeli assassination ends ceasefire."

Sometimes the popular Shimon Peres went on a media tour. He wouldn't meet the eleven Dutch correspondents in Israel, but would come to Holland. The interviews were done by domestic editors, who didn't know enough to ask him difficult questions. Intensely critical follow-up questions were impossible anyway because he only gave ten minutes to each medium.

At the beginning of the second intifadah, the Israeli army often turned their guns on stone-throwers, and aimed above the waist. Dozens of children were killed; hundreds were wounded. An Israeli PR operation managed to redirect the question from "What right does Israel have to use such violence on adolescent stone-throwers protesting against the occupation?" to "Why on earth do Palestinian parents expose their children to such danger?" The answer was in the Black Book: They hate us—look at how they are being incited.

***

Palestinians often complained about the Western media, and I came to understand why. But I saw a different reason for the distortion than they did. Many Palestinians suspected a Jewish conspiracy—sinister forces controlling the media behind the scenes. We'd get into heated discussions, and I didn't always manage to take the sting out of it with a joke—for example, by looking at my watch and saying, "Can I just make a call? My secret boss in Israel is going to dictate tomorrow's article to me."

I couldn't see any conspiracy; it was more like a number of trump cards that the Israeli government played. Not only did they have more resources, but the Israeli government also profited from the fact that the average Westerner, whatever his or her political leanings, had more sympathy for Israel. This was not so much because the country is Jewish, but because it is Western. Israel produces Western literature and films, has famous classical musicians, competes in the football Champions League, and joins in the Eurovision Song Contest. Indigenous Europeans look more like Israelis than Palestinians, and that's why Israeli suffering is easier to understand. *The New York Times*'s Opinion page often features articles from Jewish settlers about living in the shadow of terrorism. "Everyone's on a diet here because our weight is the only thing we can control," one settler wrote. An allusion like this is recognizable to Western readers who also diet from time to time.

Palestinians showed their suffering in other ways. One Gaza aid organization asked Palestinians and Western expats to select photographs that symbolized the intifadah for them. The Westerners chose morning mothers, crying children, and devastated properties; the Palestinians came up with marching men and clenched fists. I've often been to Palestinian demonstrations, and in Western PR terms they were disasters: A father shouting angrily, "Is this justice? Is this justice? My daughter was eleven! Is this justice?"—the body being carried aloft, the shots in the air, the chanting . . .

Jewish Israelis usually bury their dead with calm cere-
mony, to the accompaniment of sobbing attendants and the
composed words of a family member. Westerners understand
these images. But how can correspondents show the sorrow
hiding behind the hysterical chaos into which Palestinian
burials often degenerate? Vulnerability is not shown: Arabs
mourn at home, away from the cameras.

Israel had another trump card, and I noticed it every time I
was back home discussing the situation with colleagues. If
I ever wanted to defend Israel during such conversations, one
phrase was sufficient: The Holocaust. Most people understood immediately, and if not I added a couple of sentences
of explanation, "For more than two thousand years, Jews
have been discriminated against, persecuted, and massacred
by non-Jews, culminating in the gas chambers. Obviously the
Jewish people can only be safe when they have their own
country, and what is more logical than the place which was a
Jewish nation two thousand years ago, according to the Old
Testament?"

Then I'd try to put the Palestinian perspective across, and
ten sentences were never enough. Central to them was not the
Holocaust, but centuries-long Western interference in their
area. This began with the crusades, was advanced by colo-
nialism, and was completed by the establishment, at the heart
of the Arab world and at the cost of the people who had been
living there, of a strange, Western country—Israel.

The handicap for the Palestinians is that the crusades and
colonization are less prominent in the Western collective
consciousness than the Holocaust, and I learned that I could
only convey the Palestinian perspective by turning things

around. Imagine a lunatic becoming president of America, and rounding up and slaughtering everyone with a Friesian grandfather. [Friesia is a semi-autonomous province in the Netherlands, with its own language.] It turns into a massacre of unimaginable proportions; then, when the anti-Friesian regime finally falls, it's clear that the surviving Friesians don't want to live in America anymore. A plan is devised in which the Friesians will get their own country, and where more logical than the place that according to old documents used to be Friesian. Despite Dutch resistance, the UN votes the plan through, and people from all over the world with a Friesian grandfather arrive in the new Friesian nation, generously subsidized by America. The remaining Dutch people protest that they've never had a problem with the Friesians; but, in international public opinion, sympathy for the Friesians holds sway. A proposal is made: Half of the country will become Friesia, and the Dutch can live in the other half.

The Dutch don't accept this; there's a war, which the Friesians win with American help, and an even larger part of the Netherlands falls into Friesian hands. Hundreds of thousands of non-Friesian refugees flood into the major Dutch cities, and tensions rise, particularly because small groups of Dutch people have instigated guerrilla warfare against the Friesians. Friesian spokespeople cry "terrorism" on CNN and that "They are killing innocent Friesians!"

Meanwhile, the Dutch people are beginning to wonder what kind of leaders they have. A military coup follows, and when the Netherlands tries to get weapons from abroad, the young Friesian state takes over the rest of the Netherlands, as well as parts of Germany and Belgium, in a "preventative attack." Droves of non-Friesian Dutch people flee over the borders into Germany and Belgium, where coups follow: "We've got to prevent the Friesians from getting us." In the interim, the Friesian army governs the occupied Dutch provinces with a heavy hand, strangles the economy, and confiscates the most beautiful areas for settlements and special roads from the settlements to Friesia. A peace process follows, and the Netherlands is offered three out of the twelve Dutch provinces: Limburg, a piece of Brabant, and one of the Zeeland islands. These fragments cannot be called the Netherlands, the Netherlands is not allowed an army, and all the borders are to be guarded by Friesian troops.

One of the pitfalls of a correspondent's post in the Holy Land is becoming cynical, so in an article about the Palestinian view of the conflict I deleted the sentence: "In PR terms, the Holocaust is gold for Israel." You can't put it like that in the paper, because you run the risk of one of the survivors of the Jewish persecution reading it and taking it the wrong way. Nevertheless, the historical connection with the West gave Israel a starting point for its campaigns, and every week there I saw an example of this. Every now and then, an Arab country would buy missiles from China or Russia, and press conferences and briefings would be convened immediately in Israel. "These missiles could reach Tel Aviv!"—the implication being that there was a threat of a new Holocaust. In the meantime, Israel received billions of dollars of "military assistance" from America, giving it countless times more destructive power than all of its neighbors put together. There weren't any briefings about that.

But references to the anti-Semitism of the past could also present Israel as the underdog, as a vulnerable country that wants peace but is surrounded by "masses of Arabs" who "want to drive all the Jews into the sea." In these representations, Palestinians and Arabs were driven by the same hatred as the Nazis. All Israel wants is "a place in the sun," and the neighbors need to prove that they no longer hate the Jews. That's what makes "They are killing innocent Jews" such a brilliant quote. "They" means "All Palestinians are guilty"; "Innocent" means "The motive is hatred"; and "Jews" means "It's not about Israelis or Zionism; this is just one more slaughter of the Jews."

It was an incredibly strong message, and in many reports in the Western media one could hear the echoes of Israel as the peace-loving underdog. The record shows that Jewish groups committed bloody terrorist attacks during the British colonial occupation, in the 1948 war, and afterwards. They murdered a UN envoy, tried to blow up the British foreign minister, and chased Palestinians from their villages on a large scale, sometimes with accompanying violence. Yet Western media mostly describe these groups as "the Jewish underground." In 1956, 1967, and 1982, Israel attacked one of its neighbors, but these invasions are often labeled "preventive attacks." The occupation of South Lebanon created a "security zone" in which Israeli *Defense* Forces were "present." This army doesn't "attack" but "acts," "enters," or "intervenes." "Security forces" perform "operations" in which "elements" are "eliminated." Assassinations are "preventive military strikes," and civilian casualties are "blunders."

There was a lot of grumbling amongst journalists about the Israeli government's use of the Holocaust, but how can you ask Israel to ignore the greatest catastrophe in the history of the Jewish people? Imagine, you've got a trump card that enables you to present yourself as a vulnerable underdog in a sound bite of around ten seconds, and with which you can write off the critics who see this differently as the worst kind of scoundrels. Of course you're going to use such a trump card—especially if you think you're caught up in a life-or-death conflict.

It was all quite logical, but the cultural and historical connection between Israel and the West did bring to light a new weak spot in the showing-both-sides principle of objective journalism. What to do if, all the manipulation aside, the Israeli one-minute slot on television hit home with the public much more than the Palestinian one-minute slot did?

***

In the Holy Land, I covered the Palestinians, and that meant a lot of on-the-ground reporting. I visited a Palestinian family whose mentally handicapped son had been shot dead by Israeli marksmen. There had been a curfew—but try explaining that to their son. I visited families whose houses had been bulldozed because Jewish settlements had been fired on from their neighborhood, and listened to the lady of the household say groggily, "Go talk to the neighbors, son—they're much worse off. We were given five minutes by the Jews to get our stuff out of the house, so we still have our gold and Grandfather's medicine." In Ramallah, I met the computer nerds who made the posters honoring the martyrs and victims of the intifadah. There they were, playing around with photos of the dead and the Aqsa mosque, text boxes with dates and causes of death, and often a verse from the Koran. "If we make the Aqsa mosque a little bit smaller, we'll be able to fit in the verse."

In Qalqilya, I hung around with Palestinian IT students.

Because of the Israeli cordons around their town, they could no longer get to the university in Ramallah; they killed time looking up the credit card details of settlers online, and ordering inordinate quantities of porn for them. In Jerusalem, I spoke to Palestinians who resold settlers' cars. The latter reported their cars to the insurance companies as stolen, the cars would be driven along back roads to a Palestinian city that the Israeli police weren't allowed to enter, and were then resold there with new number plates. In Bethlehem, a gravedigger told me that he could hardly cope with demand, and in Gaza I got drunk with a Palestinian businessman whose factory had been plundered by settlers and afterwards razed by bulldozers . . . along with his stables, with his horse still in them.

Those kinds of human interest stories did well, but political news was central to this conflict. Telling both sides was part of this, and when I watched CNN I couldn't escape the impression that the Palestinian spokesmen were missing chances to make their case. I saw it happen with every political development: The periodic "visionary speech" from Washington, Israeli elections, broken-off and re-instigated peace discussions . . . A polished Israeli spokesman who rammed home a single point: Israel wants peace, but they are killing innocent Jews. Then the Palestinian spokesman: "Clearly . . . the Palestinian nation . . . will never accept the barbaric Israeli crimes . . . which are, of course, totally rejected." Tirades such as this would give no answer to the presenter's questions, and would leave viewers with confusing improvisations and incomprehensible quotes about international legitimacy.

In the beginning, I thought that the Palestinians couldn't do any better. But for my human interest stories, I often spoke to prominent Palestinians from outside the Authority—doctors, human rights activists, businessmen, academics. These were talented people, well-read, articulate, and ironic. Why didn't I see these people on CNN? I decided to ask each and every one of them whether they realized how bad their media image was, and why nothing was being done about it.

They were happy to talk about it, I noticed, and their answers nearly always began with three points: We've got less money than Israel; Westerners are racist because you consider an Israeli death to be more important than a Palestinian one; and you let yourselves be blackmailed with the Holocaust. I would patiently sit out the list and remark that this didn't explain why the Palestinians didn't make the most of the chances they did have. Then I'd ask, "Why don't I see you, instead of the spokespeople from the Palestinian Authority, on CNN?"

Often there'd be a deep sigh, followed by a hurricane of frustration. "Our authorities are incompetent and don't want to improve. They are incompetent because Arafat gave all the senior positions to confidants from his PLO period," was what nearly every prominent Palestinian said. Those confidants had lived as fugitive nomads for decades, and they had very limited experience with Western democracies. That's why spokesmen on CNN always started to talk about resolution 4-7-whatever and "international legitimacy." Western policymakers understood that they were offering peace in accordance with UN resolutions, and the Palestinian spokespersons aimed their speeches at these Western policymakers. Arafat's head honchos could not imagine that you could get your own way in a democracy by convincing the masses who elected those policymakers.

But the real problem lay elsewhere, my conversational partners emphasized. The unsuccessful media policy was a direct consequence of the authoritarian organization of the Palestinian Authority. An Israeli politician wants to be re-elected; after that, he wants to be remembered. He or she will therefore try to satisfy as many people as possible, and a clever media policy helps in this. But Arafat's first and only priority was not to be toppled from power. If a sympathetic Palestinian woman with fluent English comes across well on CNN, Western audiences want to know more about her. Newspapers and television shows come to interview her, and left-wing politicians want to be photographed with her. As she gains power, she becomes a threat to the leader. This was why the charismatic Hanan Ashrawi—a woman who had been able to eloquently defend the Palestinian perspective in the early nineties—was sidelined. This is why the Palestinian Authority thwarted mediagenic, peaceful mass demonstrations against the occupation—they might run over into protests against their own leader.

"Our spokesmen are not involved in creating effective media policy, but with keeping the leader happy," the Palestinians outside the Authority admitted through gritted teeth. In return, the state paid for their children to study at the best American universities, and their family had access to the best hospitals, enjoyed all kinds of privileges, and became world famous. They'd lose all of these things if they did too well and became a threat to the leadership. In the top echelons of the Palestinian Authority it was loyalty that counted, not competence.

Just like what had happened in the Arab world, I'd been missing something all along—the Palestinians had a dictator! The repression was not as bad as the kind their neighbors suffered, but the leader and his cronies were above the law and were primarily looking after their own interests.

The Palestinian Authority had been created with European money and American know-how after the Oslo peace agreement of 1993. Israel had also given a helping hand, and that was understandable. Every few years, Israel got a new government that could put all the treaties on hold, or reinterpret them, or apply new conditions to them; but a dictator is a dictator, and if he agrees to something, he's stuck with it. The peace process often focused on the question of what was reasonable. In Israel, the Labor Party could point at Likud and say that the Palestinian demands were simply unrealistic: "Look how much pressure we get from the opposition; if it was up to them, the Palestinians would get even less." When it was his turn, the Likud leader could point at his supporters and say that he simply couldn't concede any more, or his party would revolt.

The Palestinian Authority could never dismiss an Israeli demand like that, because there was no formal political opposition. It was all quite logical, and I understood better why Israel and Western governments, despite their rhetoric, would rather do business with dictators. A single strong man is easier to control and put the thumbscrews on than a democratically elected leader. When a dictator fights a media war with you, he will not send his best men onto the battlefield.

Chapter Ten

A Bloody Occupation

Working in the Holy Land was wonderful, because Dutch interest in it was enormous. This also had its downsides, though, and if I ever forgot them I only had to open the Letters page or, better still, the online guest books for the *NRC* newspaper or the NOS broadcasting station.

People really let fly there, and there was no way of telling who was going to be annoyed by something. Usually, I covered the Palestinians in the occupied zones, while my colleague in Tel Aviv did the Jewish Israelis and the millions of Palestinians inside Israel—the Israeli Arabs. We generally balanced each other out, but at one point my colleague went on holiday. I had just written three stories about Palestinian suffering and, thanks to it being the slow season, two of them had made the front page. I realized the reporting was becoming skewed. Why not risk my life by doing this report:

Whoever wants to know what terrorism is doing to Israel should take a bus in the worst-hit city, Jerusalem. The hydraulic door hisses open, you mount the steep steps and instantly feel the eyes on you. Is he an Arab? Is he wearing a long coat or carrying a bag? The bus driver deliberately asks you a question to find out whether you've got an Arabic accent or not.

You take a seat under a sign that says: "No smoking. No throwing rubbish out of the window." And a poster suggesting "Why not take a bus trip to the zoo!" The bus sets off and faces relax for a few minutes. The Sabbath will begin in a couple of hours and everyone is doing their shopping—an ideal time for an attack. We drive past the peddlers' market, which has been a target and which is now guarded by bored-looking agents with metal detectors, along the streets where in early March a group of Orthodox Jews were blown up, over the crossroads with Ben Jehuda where one chilly night two bombs went off in succession amongst a group of young people on a night out.

Another stop. Twelve buses have been bombed already during this intifadah. Eighty people have been killed, five hundred have been wounded and thousands of eyewitnesses have been traumatized. When asked if he keeps an eye on who gets on, soldier Menachim answers, "Always. I look to see if the person looks suspicious, tense or even just aloof." But a bomb is a bomb and even Menachim admits that a terrorist has plenty of time to press the button in the few seconds it would take to overpower him. Terrorists are getting ever more inventive and disguise themselves as ultra-Orthodox Jews, soldiers or hippies, complete with bleached hair and a guitar, containing the bomb. And since the arrival of *shahidas*—female suicide bombers—on the scene, you have to watch out for the women as well. Add to this the fact that at least a quarter of Israeli Jews are of Middle Eastern origin and therefore look very similar to Arabs and it becomes clear how much mortal fear the bus passengers endure. Why do they continue to take the bus? Menachim says that the army forces him to. "We're not allowed to hitchhike because life has to go on as if there weren't any attacks, otherwise the terrorists win." But many Israelis take the bus for another reason. The country is experiencing its worst-ever financial crisis. The rich buy cars for their children and give them extra pocket money so that they don't have to take on weekend work in pizzerias or other dangerous places. Recently the Israeli press published a list of prominent politicians who had sent their children to safety in American universities. It was a long list.

That's the only real protection—leaving the country. "Palestinian operations are a message to all Jews in the world, 'Stay where you are, don't go to Israel,'" Hezbollah reminds us on its satellite channel after nearly every attack. Hamas leader, Mahmud Zahar expresses it with cutting simplicity: "The bombs are supposed to make the Israelis so afraid that they'll leave."

Leaving is not something that many Israelis do, but they are afraid. "I feel guilty every time I get off because an Arab has got on," said one young man who preferred to remain anonymous. "But what am I supposed to do?" As we reach our final destination, Menachim asks, "Are you afraid?" When he gets an affirmative answer he nods slowly, strokes his gun and says consolingly, "There's no reason to be afraid." His smile is understanding but his eyes remain fixed on the bus door.[11]

This piece made the front page, too, and I thought that balance in the reporting had been restored. However, the pro-Israeli correspondence club *take-a-pen.org* thought differently. They keep an eye on all the media, and encourage members to write angry letters. This was what they said:

> Take a Pen friends. (. . .) What do you think about this sentence—"the only real protection against terrorist attacks is to leave the country?" Given that this isn't a quote by a bus passenger, I think he's giving away his own opinion, which neatly concurs with Hezbollah's and Hamas's goal. NRC email address: Opinie@nrc.nl. Regards,

It was followed by the name of the lobbyist. One of the members sent this reaction to the *NRC*:

> Shalom, I saw that you were getting wound up about that stupid drivel too. Don't you get it, mate? Jews should just LEAVE. Why don't those Jewish bastards get that? AWAY WITH THEM. Why do they still fail to understand this after about 4,000 years of Jorises making it obvious?

Some of the letter writers were so aggressive that I found it increasingly difficult to imagine that they had anything valuable to say. Their reasoning was often reminiscent of that of Arab regimes: Criticism of our group is forbidden because our enemies might use it, and so whoever is critical must belong to the other side. I gave a few lectures in the Netherlands; sometimes, impeccably dressed, eloquent people would come up to me afterwards. They'd wait timidly while the younger generation asked what it was like to be in a bomb attack or requested tips for their forthcoming holiday to Jordan. Then it would be their turn. "Thank you for your reading, but my husband and I sometimes have great difficulties with the things you write about Israel." You get your answers down pat, and mine was: "Are you bothered by what Israel is doing or by the fact that I am writing about it?" And then I'd get a glassy stare—he's one of *them.*

Tirades by sympathizers of the Palestinian cause were something I tended not to read either, especially if they were written by people who didn't speak any Arabic. If even 5 percent of Palestinians get further in English than "Israel is very bad," that's a generous estimate. If you care so much about the Palestinians, go and learn their language so that you know who you are supporting, I'd have thought.

The fervor was no less because of it, and it didn't help either when my boss said in a radio interview, "You can't do anything right when it comes to Israel and Palestine. If the criticism is a little balanced, we've done well." It was impressively honest of him to admit that he didn't have a position regarding the situation, and tried to adopt the middle ground; but by publicly admitting this, he encouraged the lobbyists to shout even louder and become more extreme. The more they pushed to the extremes, the greater the chance that the middle position would move with them.

In fact, there was only one group who never attacked me, who were consistent in their support, and who praised my work whether its import was more negative for "the" Arabs or "the" Jews: The neo-Nazis.

***

The disadvantage of unreasonable criticism is that it blinds you to well-considered criticism. At least, that's how I explain why it took me nearly two years to understand the criticism from the Israeli peace movement and a few other champions of the Palestinian cause. Their criticism of the media was not that presenting both sides of the story was disadvantageous to the Palestinian viewpoint; they went a step further, and criticized the underlying approach that if two sides are fighting they must both be at fault. In their opinion, the conflict should be covered the same way that the Apartheid regime in South Africa had been covered in the 1980s. Peace activists said that while violence should be denounced, and terrorism absolutely so, when people with superior military strength suppress an essentially defenseless population, that fact should be central. No one said during the Apartheid regime that when blacks and whites fought, both were wrong.

I'd heard this criticism from my first visit to the Holy Land onwards, but it had never sunk in. The reason was simple: I hadn't really understood what living under occupation was like. During the final year of my posting, this changed because I went to live in occupied East Jerusalem.

Well-meaning fellow journalists who, like nearly all correspondents, lived in Israel, told me not to go. They said I'd never cope. I simply thought that, if I moved, I'd be rid of that endless commuting between Israel and Lebanon. So off I went, and my light-hearted state of mind permeated the article I wrote about the logistical hell of moving house:

> It sometimes takes a while for you to realize you're not on
> the ball anymore. It happened to me last week when I sat in

a fancy teashop in Amman catching my breath after three hellish days of moving house. My helpmate and I ordered soup but it arrived lukewarm. I sent it back, tasted it—lukewarm. Sent it back, lukewarm again. Sent it back and still lukewarm. Come over here, I gestured to the waiter. I spooned up some soup and put his thumb in it. Feel it—lukewarm. I pointed at the teapot. That's how hot we want it.

It was not just the fact that I licked the spoon afterwards (waste not, want not), what made me wonder about my mental state was that it took me five minutes to realize how strange my behavior was. The waiter was now in the kitchen thinking, "I've always defended Westerners, but this is the last straw. If there's ever a fair election I'm going to vote fundamentalist."

We'd spent the past three days moving my things from Beirut to Jerusalem. As the crow flies that's a four-hour drive, but the border is closed and getting hold of a removal firm is tricky because Lebanon and Israel suspect every contact as espionage. You can do it via Cyprus where they repack all the stuff in new boxes and send it on, but the astonishingly corrupt Lebanese customs officials want ten dollars for every CD you export, and if the thick wad of paperwork is not in order in Israel, your belongings stay at the port and you have to pay seventy dollars a day for storage. What's more, the Israeli removal company refused to transport my belongings from the port to East Jerusalem because Palestinians live there. Welcome to the Middle East.

This was why we jammed a taxi full in Beirut and drove through Syria to Jordan. The following day we were hoping to get into Israel through the generally lax border point at the Allenby Bridge. I pictured myself faced with a strict customs official—me with my satellite telephone, gas mask, ten thousand dollars, and a passport full of stamps from sinister countries. *Mr. Bin Laden, I presume?*

The first hiccup was the Syrian border. Dutch tourists can buy visas there but not if they are journalists, and unfortunately my passport contained an expired press visa for Syria.

"Transit visa?" I asked as despairingly as possible.

"You need to get permission from the ministry and the ministry's closed."

"Twenty dollars?" I let my driver suggest.

"We'll see what we can do."

Forty dollars poorer and four hours later, but in possession of one transit visa, we drove to the real customs post. It was a tense moment because officially they are supposed to estimate the value of your possessions and take this amount in insurance. At the Jordanian border we'd get the money back. Yeah, right—as if they'd have sums like that lying around and would ever hand them out. We addressed the situation in an alternative manner, and a little while afterwards we were driving un-inspected but a hundred dollars lighter, past the snow-topped mountains of the Golan Heights. Getting out of Syria cost another hundred dollars, and then we could finally breathe because Jordan is a relatively decent country. Next, an argument with the driver over his fee, someone in the car behind us driving crazily and almost sending us into a ravine, and then the border was closed. Two Palestinian infiltrators had been caught. We were about to turn around when the border suddenly opened again.

In East Jerusalem a further setback awaited us. The Palestinian painters, plumbers, and carpenters who were supposed to do up my house hadn't been able to leave their villages for a week. We dumped all the stuff at a friend's house and returned to Beirut the following morning: Taxi to the border, thirty dollars Israeli exit tax, an hour and a half waiting for a bus, eight dollars for the Jordanian government, haggling with a new driver in order to get to the airport which had flights to Beirut. It was cold and we were hungry. You know what, we thought, if we go through Amman we can stop for a bowl of delicious, piping hot soup. We'll have earned it.[12]

Having left my Lebanese lodgings, I could no longer distance myself from the situation. This realization didn't dawn on me instantly, for right after my move I was happiness personified. Life in East Jerusalem seemed the most interesting thing ever. There I was in the queue at IKEA behind a Jewish settler with a huge beard, a gaggle of kids, a cradle under his right arm, and an automatic rifle on his left shoulder. In Israel, settlers are allowed to carry heavy weaponry. East Jerusalem was occupied territory, and there was no postal service, so I had to get a post box in the Jewish settlement close by. The Israeli telecommunications company didn't want to come and install an ISDN line; it was too dangerous amongst all those terrorists.

This was the eye of the storm, and I noticed it in the jokes. The chief rabbi is visiting the pope in Rome and needs to make a phone call to God. The pope gives him the telephone and says, "If you write down your address, we'll send you the bill later." A month later, a huge bill arrives, which the rabbi pays with a sigh. Then the pope pays a return visit to Jerusalem; he needs to call God, too. It's a long conversation and, after he hangs up, the pope asks the rabbi if he needs his contact details for the bill. The rabbi hesitates and then shrugs his shoulders: "Don't worry about it, pal. It's local rates here."

The main Palestinian bookshop in Jerusalem's Saladin Street had stuck up a cartoon: On the first picture, an angry Eskimo is saying, "My name is Menachim, and Jerusalem is MINE!" Next, an angry black man: "My name is David, and Jerusalem is MINE!" An American in a cowboy hat stamping his feet: "My name is Shimon, and Jerusalem is MINE!" A furious Russian: "My name is Shlomo, and Jerusalem is MINE!" An irate Indian: "My name is Benjamin, and Jerusalem is MINE!" The final picture has a confused-looking Palestinian: "My name is Mohammed, and I was born in Jerusalem, but it must have been some kind of mistake."

People in the Holy Land could make fun of themselves, but when did you ever see that on the news? My Israeli technician, a big Ajax fan, once complained that his dog had fleas. "I need to buy some pesticide, German stuff. They're good at that, the Germans—stamping out vermin." He also told me this one: An American, a Russian, and an Israeli are standing in front of a sign that says APOLOGIES, NO MEAT TODAY DUE TO SHORTAGES. The American asks, "What are shortages?" The Russian asks, "What's meat?" The Israeli asks, "What are apologies?"

***

It was a whole new world, and I was so happy there that I threw a house-warming party. Amongst the guests were my landlord and his sister, our neighbor. A Dutch diplomat from Tel Aviv was present, too, along with a Swedish colleague, Sven. Sven came over to me, looking quite upset. "That landlord of yours and his sister, they're . . . nice!" I raised my glass. What did he expect? "Well. Yeah. It's probably nothing, but they're . . . you know." It had been Sven's first conversation with ordinary Palestinians. Tel Aviv to East Jerusalem is a fifty-nine-kilometer drive, and there's no border crossing point because Israel has annexed East Jerusalem and considers it as part of the country; but in his three years in Tel Aviv, Sven had never come here. Instead, he'd swallowed the Israeli PR stories whole.

The landlord and his sister opened my eyes about what occupation was like, too. That was the end of my happiness. My neighbor taught me the most. She was a Catholic spinster who'd been born in Haifa in 1948. When Israel was founded, the family had fled to East Jerusalem and had never been able to go back. East Jerusalem was in Jordanian hands at the time, but in 1967 it was taken by Israel—so the neighbor ended up being ruled over by the country that had previously robbed her family of everything.

And still there was no peace for her. She received phone calls at three o"clock in the morning; each time she answered there'd be a few seconds' silence, and then they'd hang up. This went on for days until my neighbor was exhausted. Burglars? She avoided my question as to why she didn't go to the police. "I'm a helpless old lady," she kept saying. It was driving me crazy. I extended the cable so that I could answer the phone, hoping that the caller would be intimidated by a male voice. That night, the phone did indeed ring; when I picked it up, there was silence. Five minutes later, it went again; more silence, so I said the nastiest thing I could think of in English. During the third phone call, the caller suddenly began to speak in heavily punctuated English. He didn't want to say who he was or why he was calling, but introduced himself as "a friend of the family from the Jordan." He hung up after that, and I realized that he hadn't pronounced Jordan with an Arabic "r," but with a throaty Hebrew one. He was an Israeli! The phone calls stopped.

"We get a lot of phone calls like that," the landlord told me when I was paying him my rent. He was a respectable, nervous doctor in his late fifties. "Settlers intimidate elderly Palestinians, and then the frontmen come and make an offer on your house, two or three times what it's worth, and you can stay there until you die. But afterwards it becomes a settlers' house. They also offer Israeli passports, which proves that they are in cahoots with the government."

So this was the "Judaization policy" with which Israel tried to get rid of all the non-Jews living in East Jerusalem. The landlord maintained that he hadn't considered the night-callers' offers for a second. However, an Israeli passport would allow him to travel abroad. His children would be able to study in America and find partners. How many Catholic Palestinians were there still in Jerusalem? Israel was going to win the battle for my house—that much was clear.

Take the example of the time my neighbor rang my doorbell in a panic. There was a curfew that evening. Israel was celebrating its independence, and all Palestinians had to stay in—those in East Jerusalem, too, for the first time—as a "security measure." The neighbor was trembling all over; she was convinced that the same thing was going to happen as occurred in 1948. I cancelled my date ("Sorry, I'm not allowed to leave my house tomorrow"), and went to fetch food from the local supermarket. Unfortunately, a lot of people had got there first. I looked at the clock—was there still time to go to a big supermarket? But what if I went, and got stuck there? I'd have to sleep in a hotel. So I had to take my passport with me, and my computer, too, because I had a deadline to meet.

I stayed home, and an hour later the neighbor was at my door again. She'd heard that there were going to be house searches, and warned me to hide all my valuables. She had a point—try proving that a soldier has taken your jewellery at gunpoint. The curfew began, and a car screeched past outside. Was this a Palestinian daredevil or a settler? There was no curfew for Jews. Then I heard explosions, and for a second I worried about my neighbor. But it was only the fire-works display for Israel's anniversary.

Then, some time later, we were burgled. The car was stolen, the house was emptied, and the neighbor was in a state. A trip to the police station? "I want to help you," the landlord said, "but then you'd better make the report." I was very annoyed, so he reluctantly explained that, if he went to the police, there was a risk that the officer would say: "You live there? That's a neighborhood we're interested in. You don't want to tell us anything? Perhaps we should check your driving license, your medical practice permit, and other paperwork. It might take a while. Report back every after-noon for the next month, and we'll go for a walk through your neighborhood—let everyone see what good friends you are with the Israeli police."

I went alone to the police station in the nearby settlement, Neve Yaqov. No one could or wanted to speak English, and I was sent over to a policeman who spoke Arabic. He was busy with a Palestinian who lived just past a checkpoint and had to queue every day to get through, two hours out and two hours in. The Palestinian had come to get a pass so that he could use the special road for Jews. It was bizarre how quickly I got used to that kind of expression—"the special road for Jews."

"Come back tomorrow," I heard the policeman bark.

"But you said that yesterday, and the day before. I've been here ten times now."

"Then come ten times more."

What was it to be more afraid of the police than burglars? Was this occupation? I decided to ask what it was like every time I interviewed anyone, and out came the stories:

It was before the peace process. I was sixteen and in love like you only experience once in your life, with my neighbor. Then anti-Israeli slogans were daubed on our house, and a PLO flag. The next day soldiers forced my father to scrub off the graffiti. I lost my cool and got arrested. Six months later I was released, but my name was known to the Jews and I could forget about getting a work permit for Israel. I had no future, and she got married to someone else.

My eight-year-old son is deaf. We live in Jerusalem, and the only special school for the deaf is in Ramallah. But I need a special pass for those ten kilometers to Ramallah. Of course, the Jews wanted something in return. My cousin's in Hamas, and I didn't want to betray him. Now my son has to stay in lodgings in Ramallah, and I travel secretly cross-country each weekend to fetch him and bring him back. He's an anxious kid, but because of his deafness we can't even reassure him by telephoning in the evenings.

My dad's the mayor, and we had enough money for me to study in Paris. Wine, literature, protests . . . but there was always a cloud hanging over my head—if I lost my original ID card Israel would never let me back in. I was messing around with a girl once and got overcome by total panic. I had to run to my room to check whether my ID card was still where I'd put it.

It was before the peace process. My brother had a business conflict with a powerful family who were linked to the PLO. One day they enticed him out to the countryside and murdered him. After that, they wrote on all the walls that he'd collaborated with Israel. What could we do?

My father had a heart defect that they couldn't treat in Gaza. We asked for a permit to travel to Jordan, but didn't get it. We'd filled in a form incorrectly, and now my father is dead.

I had a terrible row with my youngest son yesterday. I asked him what he wanted to be when he was older, and he said "martyr." I said that a repressed people needs soldiers, but it also needs thinkers, inventors, scientists. He laughed at me. Why should he work hard at school if he can never leave Nablus to go to a good university? And he's right.

These were haunting stories, precisely because they weren't told by angry, bearded men, by incompetent spokesmen, or by theatrically weeping victims. These were calm men and women; father and mothers trying to keep their families together; grandparents who realized that the next generation could expect a life just like theirs. The only conclusion possible was that occupation is tantamount to terrorism—only it's permanent, and enforced by soldiers and secret services rather than terrorists. An occupation is like a dictatorship because you don't have any rights. The Israeli "security services" could burst into your home at any moment and take you or a family member away, and they could torture you or lock you up for years without trial. At any moment, a bulldozer could flatten your house, as collective punishment or for a new Jewish settlement.

This is how Palestinians have lived since 1967, and the peace process hasn't changed anything significant. The "Palestinian Authority" is, in fact, a layer that has been pushed between the Israeli occupiers and the population. Before the peace process, Palestinians had to ask the Israelis permission for everything; after it, they had to go the Palestinian Authority, which then had to ask permission from Israel.

Until it was stolen, I drove an imported car with a Greek number plate. Every few hours, I'd be pulled over by special anti-terrorist units—sometimes in civvies, sometimes in uniform. "From where this car?" There were often heart-stopping moments when I thanked God for my white skin because I didn't speak any Hebrew and didn't know if they were shouting "Get out of the car or we'll shoot!" or "Don't move a muscle or we'll shoot!" The policemen were extremely nervous, too: A terrorist would wait until they approached, and . . . boom. But that feeling of powerlessness when I had to raise my hands and walk towards one of those nineteen-year-old soldiers . . .

Soldiers would sometimes set up a checkpoint in front of my house, and get every Palestinian male between eighteen and forty out of his vehicle. They had to stand in the burning sun while their papers were studied and checked, sometimes for hours, and anyone who complained got a whack around the head. Unless I, with my white skin, went along to spectate—at which point they nearly always stopped hitting.

This was what Israeli peace activists meant about occupation. When I reflected on how to portray it, I understood why so few people got what the activists were talking about. The same forces were at play in occupied countries as in Arab dictatorships. There weren't any newsworthy developments to report on, which meant that, at the most, correspondents could only put something about daily life in a background feature. The news stream was always shaped by incidents. Put another way, the occupation itself was never news, but each new attack was. This meant that I could mention occupation in cross-talks or in analysis, but only as an abstraction. How would my audience in their home country—with its customer complaint lines, ombudsmen, and hardship clauses—be able to picture this? You'd have to show occupation on television with concrete examples, but that was very hard to do.

For instance, before the second intifadah, many Palestinian homosexuals used to secretly visit Tel Aviv bars. The Israeli secret service took photos of them, and then threatened to distribute them around the Palestinians' home villages if they didn't go to work for them. A story like this illustrates how ruthlessly an occupying force crushes people—but just try capturing this on film. The homosexual won't appear on television because, if his proclivities or collaboration come out, he's in for it; and the secret services will always deny everything or refer to "state secrets." At the most, you'll get an Israeli human rights activist to talk about it. Hardly gripping.

For every bomb, you had one image that gave the essence of the situation according to Israel. The image of a burned-out bus or blackened restaurant could be endlessly repeated, and each time the message was clear within two seconds—this is terror. But occupation . . . it didn't get any further than shots of tanks, soldiers checking papers, and long queues of civilians. How could correspondents portray the misery, repression, and injustice behind such scenes? You could only *recount* this and, as we know, the most you can do with words is get something into your viewer's heads; if you've got images of an attack, you can get them in the guts.

In the first three years of the second intifadah, more than three times as many Palestinian civilians died from Israeli violence than vice versa—and still the talk was of "the bloody attacks," rarely of the "bloody occupation." After a Palestinian attack with six Israeli victims, "tensions were rising" in the Middle East; but a week in which fifteen Palestinian civilians died due to Israeli violence was brushed aside as "a period of relative calm." The Palestinian Authority had to continually explain whether it was "doing enough against terrorism." Israeli politicians never had to explain if they were "doing enough against the occupation." On the BBC website, surfers discussed "how to stop terror"; there was no forum on "how to stop the occupation."

If you compared terror with occupation, things were so skewed that you couldn't straighten them out, not even in the newspapers. I could write "humiliation," but a word like that didn't mean anything—at least it hadn't to me until I experienced it firsthand. When I did experience it, I wrote the following article. A reader wrote in angrily that I'd crossed "journalistic boundaries." He was right, because "humiliation" isn't something you can explain within journalistic boundaries:

> I was kneeling before a full toilet bowl when a hand passed me a fork and I had to pick turds out of the water and eat them, to much hilarity. I'd had this nightmare last year and

I'd forgotten it, as is typical with dreams, but yesterday I was at a roadblock and the dream came back in full detail.

It was a completely ordinary roadblock, a long queue of Palestinian cars facing four Israeli soldiers of around eighteen years old with trendy haircuts and the latest mobile phones. One of the soldiers repeatedly signaled cars in the early evening dusk with a torch bigger than his forearm. All male passengers had to get out and bare their chests to the cold wind in order to prove that they weren't hiding a bomb. The other soldiers kept the remaining passengers in the car—older women and small children—covered by their hypermodern weapons.

Finally one Palestinian had had enough. He started off by obligingly lifting up his jumper, but once he'd turned around he dropped his trousers, to the great hilarity of the Palestinians waiting in their cars. When he'd got back in his car, the man with the giant torch had him wind down his window, gave him three blows to the head, and gestured for him to drive on.

That was when I remembered my nightmare. The day before, I'd been to Jenin with a Palestinian associate. When we went to leave the city, we got stuck at an Israeli roadblock where it turned out that my associate should never have been admitted. We were starving and desperate for the loo, but the soldiers made us wait for two hours. After that we could drive on, without explanation. At least that's what we thought. Two hundred meters further up there was another roadblock; this time, the border police. "But the army have just let us through," we said. "Call them, or we can go back there with you." The policeman walked off and we half froze to death in the bitter December cold for another two hours, pacing up and down with our arms behind our backs. What do you do at such a time? Go along with it and crack jokes or, alternatively, kick up a scene with the risk that my associate could be sent to "administrative detention"—the Israeli PR term for imprisonment without trial—for six months or more? You can go now, the policeman nodded to me. Finally we could drive on, yet again without explanation. The whole way back my usually cheerful associate remained silent while I tried to sort out my feelings.

Yesterday at the roadblock I understood what those feelings had been and how my unconscious has translated them—humiliation. The kind of experience I had in Jenin only happened to me once, but imagine what it would be like to be browbeaten by Israeli kids for thirty-five years? After a while, it must result in more than just angry dreams.[13]

***

And now another joke: Two Israelis are sitting on the beach in Tel Aviv, reading. One has got a quality newspaper; the other, an anti-Semitic rag. "Why on earth are you reading that?" the one asks. "I used to read a quality newspaper like you," the other says, "but I couldn't handle it anymore—the suicide bombers and weapons of mass destruction and the collapsing economy and anti-Israel demonstrations in Europe . . ." He points to the anti-Semitic rag. "Now that I read this, I feel much better. It turns out that there's a Jewish global conspiracy and we actually control the whole world."

Chapter Eleven

The Middleman's Dilemma

Even the Holy Land has its quiet periods when there's not much news, and one of the human interest stories you can use as a potential filler is the Jerusalem syndrome. It's a condition that has been written about in serious medical journals. The long and short of it is that dozens of tourists visiting Jerusalem's Old City become gripped by the idea that the Messiah is coming. The majority of them can return home after a few days of nursing, but others spend years lodging in hostels around the place where the Messiah is supposed to appear. I wanted to know what kind of people they were, and looked up the owner of one of the hostels. "It's very simple," he said. "My guests have a problem. They can't solve it themselves, and have invested their hope in the idea that someone else can—the Messiah." The owner was a sensible man who, when I asked about his faith, answered: "My parents are Muslim." His gaze went to the guest list where some people had signed in as "the prophet Yesaya," and he muttered, "If I was the Messiah, I wouldn't be happy with followers like that."

It was difficult not to think of the Jerusalem syndrome when I followed discussions about peace in the Middle East on the Internet or via the satellite dish. Everyone seemed caught up in this syndrome—not only Arabs, but also Jews and Westerners. It was always the case that *someone else* had to do something because *someone else* was the problem; if *their* behavior improved, everything would get better. Ordinary Palestinians looked to their leaders, to Arab countries, Europe, or America—on Arabic channels, it was always Western policy that needed to change. Israel explained away its problems with the rest of the world as anti-Semitism. And, since 9/11, an increasing number of Western commentators kept saying, "Islam needs to go through an Enlightenment, Muslims need to do this, or that."

Seeing everyone abdicating their responsibilities wasn't very hope-inspiring, but during my final year as a correspondent I sometimes wondered whether I was any different. Should I try to counterbalance any distortions I came across? If a football team has won a match 8–1, you might say that a TV journalist should show the goals, and that's all. The losers should simply have played better.

But what if the pitch was sloping, one of the linesmen was a relative of the winning team, and some of the fouls were hardly penalized, or not at all, because the winning team was much better at hoodwinking the referee? What if the losers' coach was there against the will of many of the fans, or had even been hired with the help of the other team? Arafat, at any rate, had been designated "exclusive representative of the Palestinian people" by Israel and the West, at the expense of the democratically inclined leaders of the first intifadah. Europe, America, and Israel helped him to build up his "security apparatus" (the terminology!) for years so that he could kick all the rival coaches out of the game.

Shouldn't correspondents look beyond the scores and show why the team had under-performed and how it might play if other players were brought in? A journalist who limits himself to the role of middleman is actually siding with the team that is best able to influence the news cycle.

This was more than an abstract question in the ethics module, worth two points in a degree in communication studies. In a media war, journalistic approaches have political consequences. I saw that happen during the biggest media onslaught I've ever witnessed—the failure of the peace negotiations at Camp David. In the summer of 2000, the then leaders Barak and Arafat spoke over peace. The negotiations faltered, and the Israeli government immediately put forward a well-prepared story: With "unprecedented generosity," Barak had offered to give back more than 95 percent of the occupied zones; the Palestinian rejection of this proved that they had never wanted peace in the first place—their only goal was to destroy Israel. Shortly thereafter, the second intifadah broke out, and it was seamlessly incorporated into the story: Now they're fighting openly. Palestinian spokesmen could do no better than offer improvisations about "barbaric Israeli crimes" and "international legitimacy"—the familiar babble.

Approximately one year later, an American former policy-worker released details about Camp David. The "95 percent" turned out to have been a misleading calculation, because East Jerusalem and the areas around West Jerusalem were not counted as occupied zones. The 5 percent that Israel would have hung onto was made up of strips of land that ran right through Palestine. The Palestinian city would have become a patchwork cloth rather than an inhabitable area, because the borders, too, would have remained in Israeli hands. As a diplomat commented, "Prisoners control 95 percent of a jail, too."

This was the "unusually generous offer" that the Israeli government had made, but the Palestinian spokespersons had never explained their leader's rejection of it, let alone given their own version of Camp David. The consequence was that many Israeli peace activists became deflated—if Palestinians wanted peace, why had they turned down Israel's unusually generous offer?

The inadequate representation of the Palestinian perspective had political consequences, and it was not an isolated incident. In the spring of 2002, the Arab League offered Israel complete peace in exchange for a total withdrawal from the occupied zones. There was a hidden catch (providing for the Palestinian right of return), but it was the first time in history that the league had made such an offer. That same evening, Hamas made the headlines with a large attack on Israel, and after that the American and Israeli governments shut up shop on the Arab Peace Initiative, as it came to be known. The Israelis didn't address the catch or come up with a counter-offer; instead, they completely ignored it. Without a powerful media lobby in the West, the Arab lands couldn't get the offer back on the agenda. It disappeared from the Western news cycle, and Hamas got free rein in the Arabic media—if Israel and the West wanted peace, why had they ignored this offer?

At times like these, you saw the gulf between East and West, and between Israel and Palestine, widen. Should I have intervened and said that the Israeli spokesperson was spinning the facts? That the Palestinian spokesperson might be incomprehensible, but what he wanted to say, and what he meant by "international legitimacy," was this . . . ?

You could go a level deeper still. It was often said that the conflict was irresolvable, and that Jews and Muslims were destined to fight. But why did they get on for more than a thousand years then? In the Middle Ages, the only place a Jew was reasonably safe (apart from the Netherlands) was in the Islamic world. Right up to the middle of the twentieth century, there were millions of Jews living in the Arab world, in Turkey, and in Iran. The technology to build gas chambers was readily available, but the Muslims never built them.

When talking to ordinary Palestinians and Israelis, I always noted how they talked about each other in near-identical terms: "They hate us."

"All right," I'd say. "Do you hate them, too?"

"Of course not," the answer would come back. "We want peace."

I didn't get this answer ten times, nor even a hundred times, but every single time I asked one side if it hated the other. The problem seemed to be that nobody dared to show their fear, not wanting the other side to think that they were weak. This led to a downward spiral in which one party's self-defense was interpreted by the other party as aggression, thus confirming their anxieties, and so on.

If you wanted to break the cycle, you'd have to practice a radically different kind of journalism. The media wouldn't limit itself to scores like 8–1, and neither would it give an account of why one team had lost so badly. Instead, the media would explain how those twenty-two players had come to see themselves as divided into two teams and what could be done about it. You wouldn't have one angry spokeswoman on behalf of one side, faced with an angry spokeswoman on behalf of the other; instead, you'd have somebody from the peace movement. One violent incident would be set, not against another violent one in which victims and perpetrators swapped roles, but against an inspiring story about the 99.99 percent of Palestinians and Israelis who hadn't committed any violence that day.

Fear can be a self-fulfilling prophecy, but so can hope and trust. What would happen if the news stopped showing fear-inducing spectacles, in favor of mundane things that inspired hope and confidence? And how many people would keep blowing themselves up if they knew that no one would get to hear of their sacrifice, because the media would ignore it?

Yet I never tried to offer a counterbalancing view, and only once have I written something about it for the opinion pages. There were three reasons I held back. The first is my own view of journalism: If I wanted to change the world instead of showing it, I should hand in my notice and become an activist. I know fellow journalists who have done that, just as I know activists who have made the opposite step. "Everything starts with the media," they said. "We're secondary to that."

This comment showed how little some activists know

about how the news industry works. That was the second reason I didn't make adjustments or offer a counterbalance: It was almost impossible to do so. The common idea about correspondents is that they "have the story," but the reality is that the news is a conveyor belt in a bread factory. The correspondents stand at the end of the conveyor belt, pretending we've baked that white loaf ourselves, while in fact all we've done is put it in its wrapping.

Take those television clips where the correspondent like me is providing a voiceover: "Another bloody day in the Middle East. Israel killed five Palestinians suspected of terrorism. According to the Palestinian Authority, they were ordinary policemen." The editors and not the correspondent would have made the decision to run something on this particular item. The news agencies have given them a ready-made story with introductory text, images, and filling. The editors have a meeting about it, and only then do I get a call. I can propose subjects myself, but they decide on them, and their accompanying images are primarily based on the themes chosen by the news agencies and CNN.

I had one platform on which I could tell my own version to the general public: The cross-talk item on the television news. "Over to our correspondent in Jerusalem. Joris, what are the consequences for the peace process?" I'd discuss the questions asked in these conversations beforehand so it was possible to steer them. However, the editor-in-chief made sure that my story was linked to the news—and how much can you tell in three forty-five-second slots? A newspaper reader might stare at the ceiling, reflect, re-read, reflect again, and read on. On the all-powerful medium of television, everything is thrown at you at once, and seven minutes of the same talking head doesn't hold anyone's attention—not even that of the talking head himself. You can revise a written text, show it to a colleague, or even abandon it. In a cross-talk, you have to get everything right on your first attempt, off the top of your head, even while you're aware that the public has no background knowledge about the subject, and that an ill-chosen tie or a slip of the tongue might be so distracting that your entire point is lost. You also know that lobbyists and angry letter-writers are sitting in front of the TV with their notepads and DVD recorders at the ready.

My television colleagues said that a good cross-talk was a question of practice and that I had to learn how to bring things back to their essence. But that's exactly what the fight in this media war is about. Is the essence of the problem occupation or terror? Is the war about Jewish security or Palestinian freedom? I became practiced, indeed, but this consisted of accepting that I could say how many people had been blown up that day, but not why.

The third reason I didn't try to even things out was the most important: I no longer understood the situation myself. It seemed to me that Israel was taking home nearly all the Oscars every month in this media war, and you might say that I should have offered a counterbalance to that supremacy. There were always prominent compatriots in politics or in the Dutch media who were prepared to explain the events in Israel's favor. If the Labor Party won the election, Israel had opted for peace; if Likud won, then, because it was so hardline, it would be able to deliver peace. I regularly came across things like this in articles: "My heart is with the Jewish people, but I also think that a *solution* has to be found for the Palestinians." I rarely heard the opposite: "My heart is with the Palestinians, but I also think that a solution has to be found for the Jews." Discussing Israel's right to exist is practically taboo in the Netherlands, whereas the question of whether the Palestinians should have a state is perfectly acceptable.

My initial impression was that the Netherlands was pro-Israel. But in my final year as a correspondent I heard prominent Dutchies comparing Israel to the Nazis, and a major survey in Europe showed that a large percentage of those questioned considered Israel to be "one of the greatest dangers to world peace." What was this all about? What was the main distortion in the Holy Land, actually—the media moves of the Israeli regime, or the disproportionate focus on Israeli human rights violations, which apparently gave people the idea that really horrific things were happening in the Holy Land?

So for once, after yet another comparison had been made to the Nazis, I wrote that angry opinion piece. I really needed to vent my belief that this comparison was totally beside the point and only increased existential fear amongst Israeli Jews—look, those goys are at it again. I was also worried that my own work had contributed to the image of Israel as the nastiest state in the Middle East. I'd written pages and pages listing Israeli outrages, but the far greater repressions and massacres perpetrated by dictators in neighboring regions were hardly represented, or were heavily filtered.

That's why I felt the need to point out that the Nazis murdered more Jews per month than the total Palestinian civilian death-toll in half a century; that the Israeli regime has never tried to wipe out Palestinians; that the Israeli press and politicians do indeed "dehumanize" Palestinians and set them apart as an inferior group of people; but that, equally, the million Palestinians living in Israel enjoy more of the rule of law than Arabs living anywhere else in the region. Israel broke the rules, but the Arab dictators didn't have any rules. You were better off being a Palestinian under Israeli rule than a Kurd under Saddam, or a South Sudanese under the Khartoum regime.

It was a big article, and I regretted it right away. Not only did it engender angry reactions: "What right does your correspondent think he has to diagnose existential fear in the hearts of 'the' Jews?" At a dinner party, a columnist slapped me on the back and said, "That comment you wrote about Palestinians having more rights in Israel than in any other Arab world was very useful to me. Good work!" I blanched, and said that I'd written about the legal certainty of Israeli Arabs, not about Palestinians in occupied areas. But the man didn't listen at all. The media war was a game for him, his standpoint was fixed, and he was looking for arguments in support of it.

It didn't make much difference, because I'd already handed in my notice. I was just waiting for my dessert after those five exciting years—the American invasion of Iraq.

Chapter Twelve

Absurd and Bizarre

Arabs talk about the straw that breaks the camel's back; the Dutch, about drops into a bucket of water. I didn't have a breaking point, but all of a sudden felt I'd had enough, and I decided to stop. After all these years, I wanted to live in my own country again for a while. Someone from the editorial team asked why—couldn't I handle it anymore? My answer was no.

That wasn't it. Or perhaps it was. What I couldn't handle anymore was that I was getting better at handling it. The Holy Land confronted me with screaming injustices, absurdities, and mortal fear. In the beginning, I was deeply concerned about them; but after a while that wore off. Then I found my being used to it unacceptable for a while—until that wore off, too, and in a moment of clarity I asked myself how numb I was prepared to become.

Early on, I'd been very shocked in the Holy Land. I was angry about the iron-cast resistance of many Israelis to seeing themselves as perpetrators, too; about the racism against the Arabs; the hysterical nationalism that the Jewish state displayed now and again . . . I was also angry about the fact that Palestinian television endlessly repeated images of toddlers shot to pieces, that Hamas's handicraft department reconstructed in Nablus the pizzeria which had just been blown up in Jerusalem, complete with papier-mâché bodies. That whole cult around suicide bombers—how could you believe that someone who'd done that would go to heaven?

I found it disgusting, at first. But then I got used to it, just like I'd gotten used to not even noticing the beggars of my father's age in the Arab world, the lies of the regimes, or the habit that Egyptian journalists had of calling homosexuals "deviants." To be sure, my interaction with ordinary Arabs was always good; and, in terms of the cost of living, my salary was excellent. There I was, enjoying luxury and freedom in the heart of poverty and repression. I found that objectionable; but after a while that feeling wore off, which was what was really objectionable.

You even get used to the feeling of alienation. I often had the impression that I was stepping in and out of parallel worlds: My conception of reality, the Palestinian conception, the Israeli conception, and that of the Western media. My filler words changed, unnoticed, from "foolish" and "crazy" to "absurd" and "bizarre." Two particular experiences stood out.

Israel regularly set up roadblocks inside Palestinian areas.

The newsreader would say something like, "Following the attacks, Israel immediately stepped up security measures"—accompanied by images of soldiers inspecting Palestinian identity cards. I often stood and watched one of those road-blocks in my own street. Palestinian cars would queue up, sometimes for hours. However, once a car reached the head of the line, the Israeli soldiers didn't even look inside it. The boot wasn't inspected, nor any other place where a terrorist might hide a bomb. Pedestrians could also go through without showing their ID. And it got crazier still. While part of "the" traffic was stuck in a long, snaking queue at the checkpoint, another part cut through the area next to it. Here the drivers weaved through small alleyways, which led to congestion. Ultimately, both routes would take just as long; it was easy to compare them, because the not-so-secret detour came out a hundred and fifty meters behind the checkpoint, in full sight of the Israeli soldiers and of me.

These were the "security measures" that disrupted the lives of ordinary Palestinians—sometimes with deadly con-sequences, because ambulances would get stuck, too. I end-lessly described the true reality of these checkpoints; but as long as the news agencies reported on roadblocks as "security measures," the editors of all-powerful television news pro-grams continued to see and to broadcast to the world through that distorted lens.

I sometimes went for walks around Ramallah to take in the atmosphere. Were there any expensive cars on the street? Was there a lot of traffic? What kind of looks did people give you? On one of those walks, I went past the City Inn hotel. I'd been there quite often, but always in the context of "clashes between Palestinian stone-throwers and the Israeli army." Now it was deserted. At that time, no Israeli soldier could enter Ramallah, and the City Inn hotel stood on the municipal border. I don't know which came first but, suddenly, in quick succession, Israeli jeeps appeared—they must have had to leave their barracks specially to do so—and then Palestinian schoolboys, quite a long walk from their school. A few spectators turned up, an ambulance, a falafel stand, and a camera crew. Then the boys began to throw stones, and the Israelis fired into the air. The boys dared to go closer, and the Israeli soldiers shot one of them down—with the ambulance wailing, the boys chanting, and the cameras rolling.

Hello, everybody! Were the cameras there because something was happening, or did something happen because the cameras were there? I sometimes felt like I was working for *Spy TV* or *Candid Camera*. The producers and the viewers know something that the people being filmed don't, and that's funny. The news in the Middle East was like that, too, except with a forty-five degree rotation. Now the producers and the players were in view, and the joke was on the viewers at home. In Arab dictatorships, correspondents weren't open about the things they didn't know; but in Israel and Palestine, correspondents kept their mouths shut about the things they did know. In any case, I never read or heard a statement such as, "The Israeli government suggested we use this settler on-air" or "This surviving relative has been provided to us by the Palestinian Authority."

I couldn't get upset about it anymore, just as that feeling of powerlessness became quite ordinary. People in the Holy Land were suffering. I noticed it in the way they crossed the street, in their blank stares on the bus, by the way they rammed their shopping trolley into yours . . . or by how elderly Jewish ladies hobbled to cross the street when an Arab-looking man approached, or Palestinian schoolchildren hid their fear when an Israeli helicopter flew over, because fear was not cool. The faces of so many people were screaming for a solution, and I couldn't do anything. Others—settlers, peace activists, fundamentalists from both religions—worked hard on their solutions. They all knew what had to happen, and saw it as their God-given duty to push as hard as they could; and the harder one element pushed, the harder the opposing element pushed back. It was exhausting for a while, but then I got used to it.

People react to threats by fighting or fleeing, but journalists take neither tack; this meant that I had to negate reality and some of the signals my brain was sending. I went about my business like an overworked policeman ignoring a problem neighborhood. It works for a while, but the lawlessness inevitably spreads from street to street until the whole city is affected. It must have happened like that to me, too. First, I stopped feeling my fear; but when the threat continued, other parts of my emotional apparatus were affected. A friend in Lebanon told me that the civil war had permanently disrupted his "sense of reality." He told me, "In order to survive, you have to convince yourself that reality is different from what it is. That works and you survive. But how do you then find out what that reality was . . . and is?"

In the year that I lived there, more journalists were killed in the Holy Land than anywhere else. I checked my blood type, and learned new English words such as shrapnel, stray bullets, and "war-risk insurance"—the policy didn't pay out for "war damage," so you had to pay hundreds of euros a day in top-up insurance. I got a bullet-proof vest and a helmet but, well, you know how it is. Those things are dead heavy, and soon I did the same as most of my fellow journalists—when the cameras were rolling I'd put on my helmet and vest, and afterwards I'd quickly drop them off in the car. I felt like such a monkey walking around in them amongst the Palestinians, none of whom wore any protection.

This was how I pulled through the violence. I now see that I was making out as if the bullet-proof vest wasn't necessary, as though everything was a show, an amateur dramatics production in which I had to improvise. It was a mind game I continued to play, whatever happened, and quite a lot did.

I'd been living in my new house in East Jerusalem for a few weeks when a crossroads just 150 meters outside my house was bombed. The target was a bus stop at which Jewish settlers had been waiting for the regular service to their home district. I stood there watching the havoc from my rooftop—a gin and tonic in one hand, the mobile telephone in the other, on the line to the studios: "What did you say? Right in front of your door? Hang on, I'll ask the chief . . . He says that if there are a lot of casualties we'll do something on it, probably after six-thirty; it depends on whether that parliamentary debate overruns . . . damn, sorry, someone else is calling. That'll be Jakarta—good luck, eh."

A couple of weeks later, another bomb went off in the area, and a month later the same crossroads was targeted again. The first time, the bomber was the only one who died, and twenty-five people were wounded. This time, seven Israelis were killed, along with the bomber, and my neighbor found a hand in his garden. "Get out of there," you might think; but, instead of packing my bags, I studied the behavior and rituals that went with such an attack, just like an anthropologist would.

It began with a second of silence, the survivors' shrieks,

and then almost instantly the sound of sirens from every point of the compass, as if the city itself was screaming out in pain. Usually the people from Magen David Adom, "the Red Star of David," would be the first on the scene. These Jewish Red Cross volunteers would lay colored strips next to the wounded so that the medical teams knew who to treat first. Green was for the slightly wounded; yellow was badly wounded; red was critical; and black was dead. "You have to decide in a split second who you are going to try to save," one of them told me. "And who you're not." The police would screen off the bodies while the spokesmen who'd arrived at lightning speed gave their great quotes to the camera teams who'd also arrived at lightning speed. Next, a handful of chanting activists would arrive: "Death to the Arabs, may the army win, no Arabs means no terrorism." Once all these people had returned home for their dinner, the Zakah people would arrive, a Jewish organization of volunteers who would scour the vicinity for organs, limbs, and even bloodspots, and bury them according to the laws of their religion. The infrastructure service would clear up the remaining traces at breathtaking speed and so thoroughly that the following day you could drive past without spotting a thing.

Why didn't I leave? In his book *From Beirut to Jerusalem*, the *New York Times* correspondent Thomas Friedman discusses the bloody Lebanese civil war. He describes a chic dinner in which the hostess asks, "Shall we eat now or wait until the ceasefire?" War and terrorism become normal: You give them a place in your life and you carry on, because that's what everyone else is doing. Friedman said that this was why the Lebanese didn't leave when limbs went on flying through the air for years on end—the limbs of people who'd all said the same thing that morning to their partners, "Don't worry about me, darling. You know I'm always careful."

Being careful—as if that had any effect. But I was always on my guard; if I didn't watch out, I did little else. A single siren was a heart attack; two, a traffic accident; three, an attack. Traffic: Avoid the buses, because if you were next to one at a traffic light, you'd be right next to a potential bomb. Open spaces: Does anyone look Arabic? Is anyone wearing a long coat that could hide a bomb? Is that an abandoned bag? Do I still have my own bag? If you leave anything unattended in Israel you'll soon see a special robot blow up your shopping behind a quickly erected barrier. It becomes so automatic that during one short trip back to the Netherlands, I went up to the security guard at the department store entrance to have my bag checked.

The danger had me permanently on my guard but, paradoxically, I became less and less aware of it. I knew that people were dying each day, but I learned to bargain with the Grim Reaper. This gave me my sense of control and safety back—as long as I didn't really think about it, of course. Should I drive home from Ben-Gurion airport along the road through Israel that is sometimes jammed for hours, or should I take the road for Jewish settlers that goes right through the occupied zone? That one is quicker, but there are Palestinian snipers around who don't check first to see whether it's a Jewish settler driving the car—they'll find out later on the news. On the other hand, what are the chances of my car being shot at? Should I get a taxi to the beach in Tel Aviv, or take the ten-times-cheaper bus, knowing that there is a 0.0001 percent chance of it being blown to smithereens? Should I go to the Palestinian shop that often doesn't have things and is expensive, or to the cheaper Israeli supermarket where they've got everything, but which has a minuscule chance of being a target?

That was the numb state I got myself into, and everyone had their own way of achieving it. A friend, a theoretical physicist, once invited me to dinner in Jewish—and thus unsafe—West Jerusalem. How should a tough correspondent respond to that? He sensed my hesitation, and reassured me that he knew what he was doing. We drove through West Jerusalem, and when we passed a restaurant with enormous windows right next to the road he shouted, "That place is death! Look, it's so easy to get into—people who eat there must be suicidal!" According to him, terrorists had a list of places with blow-up potential. "One of their guys drives around noting down targets. Well, that restaurant has got a star!" He listed his criteria for a safe meal: The place should be well tucked away, and the doorkeeper should be at a good distance from the diners, otherwise the terrorist would just throw himself at him. It helps if Israeli Arabs eat there, too, and basements and enclosed spaces should be avoided—an explosion that can't "get out" carries on reverberating, which is the reason that terrorists prefer narrow alleyways to squares. As we ate, my friend told me casually, after an hour and a half of discussing football, women, and the laws of gravity, that the week before he'd had a coffee in his local café, had paid and left, heard a rumble and turned round, and it had been blown up. "I wasn't expecting that," he said. "But it was logical. The prime minister's office is in the area—they wanted to send a message. I should have thought of it."

Everything was different in the shadow of terrorism, but then again it wasn't; looking back on it, that was what was most alarming. Despite the permanent threat, I'd had the same trivial thoughts as always. Would the butcher have any chicken fillets left? Had I offended the ambassador's wife with my drunken behavior? Had that garage owner screwed me? The topic of conversation at an expat party could slip seamlessly from sports to tips about hidden restaurants, a back road that never had any snipers along it, or the café with new security *and* the best latte in town. You didn't call to say you'd survived an attack, because the network would be down afterwards, but text messages would get through. There was the same tone as in Amsterdam, and the same inclination to trump the other guests with the latest hot tips. And yet there was also an ever-present anxiety, which everyone denied. I was just as enthusiastic in my denial, and it carried over to my work.

There was that time in Rafah in the Gaza Strip. I can still picture myself nodding at my colleague as he cried out angrily: "We're getting out of here. We're getting out of here NOW!" Yes, yes, I nodded again, just let me finish this phone call—you know how difficult it is to get an international connection in Gaza. But the gunshots close by got so noisy that it became impossible to hold a telephone conversation anyway, and I had to hang up. Only then did I realize what was going on: There was a shoot-out going on, twenty-five meters away. Naturally, we knew that Palestinian fighters and Israel border troops often "came to blows" here, even during the daytime. That's what we'd come for, and there were signs of it everywhere—bulldozed Palestinian houses, bullet holes, and rocket strikes . . . I'd seen it so often in television dramas that I just couldn't imagine that, amongst these concrete ruins, Palestinian men my own age were trying to shoot their Israeli peers in the watchtowers just further up, and vice versa.

Real bullets were flying about, but the people in the

vicinity didn't seem to be bothered—if they weren't running away, it obviously wasn't dangerous, and I could just finish my call. My colleague, though, let his fear show, and was shaking all over. The local kids fetched him a chair, and showed him all the stickers they'd got from the foreign camera teams they'd met. Then they got bored, and began to imitate my colleague's quivering lip. One of the children shouted "Boo!" and the rest of them pulled frightened faces: "Oh, how scary!"

I tried to get through to the paper again, because it was going to be impossible to write my article, and they had to know that. I tend to pace up and down when I'm on the phone and, because the shooting had died down, I nearly walked back onto the battlefield. "No, mister!" they shouted.

The violence came even closer. At the peak of the largest wave of attacks ever to hit Jerusalem, I would only go to the Jewish part of town when I had to do live cross-talks for TV. That was how, on a clear evening on April 1, I found myself within a few meters of an attack. Immediately afterwards, I sought refuge in denial and immediately called the newsroom to say I'd probably be late for the live Q&A segment. I jumped into a taxi and focused on what we were going to discuss—I'd requested we didn't mention this bomb. I was on time, and my colleagues back home said that I didn't come across any differently than usual. Afterwards, I went off to get drunk with a few NOS associates in a hotel in East Jerusalem. The initial shock wore off, and I returned to downplaying things with quips like, "There's a bomb behind you . . . April Fool!" or joking about the fact that Palestinians call an unsuccessful attack a "falafel bomb," and that the

Dutch refer to Ben Yehuda Street as *Ben Op Je Hoede* ("Be on Your Guard") Street.

Over the days that followed, I told other journalists about it, and with each retelling of the experience it disappeared further over the horizon—so much so that I can no longer call to mind the person I was when I typed out these notes on my computer:

> I'm in a taxi bus full of Palestinians. We're approaching the crossroads with east and west, where the wall once stood across which Jordanian and Israeli snipers fired at each other. Doesn't matter. You can turn right at the crossroads, into west Jerusalem. And you can turn left, into the walled old city. We stop at a red light. I see a boy running away from a car; he's running fast. I mean, running away fast. That's odd, I think to myself, someone running so fast. Should I say something to the driver? Oh, an Israeli policeman is going over to the car. Boom. I pictured myself watching a film, at the cinema or at home on the sofa with crisps and beer and a joint to get nicely pie-eyed. The bang was different, duller and less echoey; the fireball was the same. Did the roof fly up in the air, or did I just imagine it later? I still see the policeman walking over, not understanding, his shoulders slightly back, his weapon tightly gripped. He's dead, it was in the paper, my fellow bus passengers were right when they'd commented "*rah isshurti*"—that policeman's had it.
>
> You reconstruct it. That world champion sprinter was supposed to drop the terrorist off in the midst of shopping Israelis. They ran into a police checkpoint at the crossroads. They pull over, the terrorist stays in his car, waits until a policeman comes over and, "What does this button do?"

Because he's still in the car, the bodywork absorbs the blast, and our bus seven meters away is hardly damaged. Otherwise I might be in a wheelchair now, or under the ground.

Even after that experience, I didn't return home. I became more careful, but that wore off over the course of the following year. Living and working in a war zone is like the proverbial hot bath. You keep adding hot water, and after a while it's hotter than anything you'd ever climb into, but you're already in it.

PART III

Chapter Thirteen

New Puppets, Old Strings

If America hadn't invaded Iraq, I may never have begun writing a book about filters, distortion, and manipulation in media representation. But the Iraqi war showed up a filter that I hadn't spotted until then, and because of it a lot of things suddenly fell into place. The run-up to the war was a replay of my earlier experiences in the Arab world and the Holy Land, played on fast-forward. The puppets had new names, but the strings attached to them were familiar.

The fact that the filtering, distortions, and manipulations of previous years were not incidents, but formed a pattern, became clear to me in Kuwait. The U.S. army was busy building up the troops there that would invade Iraq within a couple of weeks. I arrived at my hotel in the middle of the night, zapped through the channels, and immediately spotted a familiar kind of bias in the language. Was I in Iraq's nineteenth province, or in the British designated mini-state of Kuwait (Arabic for "small fort")? CNN and Arabic stations both mentioned the Gulf War, but how many had there been, actually? The region itself began the count with the Iran-Iraq War of the 1980s; then came the Iraqi invasion of Kuwait in 1990, with the American liberation six months later—which made this the Third Gulf War. But CNN spoke of the Second, because America hadn't been involved in the Iran-Iraq War.

Word choice meant perspective, and this was neatly illustrated in the text boxes under the images that sum up the situation in three or four words. Hezbollah had "the attack on Iraq"; America's Fox News placed the invasion within the context of the "war on terror"; CNN used "Strike on Iraq"; and Iraqi television devoted itself to the "Ultimate War." The viewers of each different channel believed that the labels they saw offered the true essence of the conflict. Each group of true believers must have thought it was great that things were being reported objectively at last.

The positioning of the chess pieces in this war also reminded me of the Holy Land. America had as much military superiority over Iraq as Israel had over the Palestinians, but wiping Baghdad from the map over the course of a morning was not possible—first, public opinion around the world had to be brought round. This was another media war, but on a larger scale, as I discovered the next morning in the press center that the U.S. army had set up in the Sheraton Kuwait City. I took my place on an uncomfortable folding chair among about a hundred and fifty fellow reporters; then a fully versed, confident army spokesman stepped up and ran through all the latest developments with a big smile. Most of my colleagues hoped to get into Iraq as embedded journalists within an American army unit, and they'd come to the Sheraton to learn whether there were any concrete details available. Unfortunately, the army couldn't say anything yet, the PR official said affably, let alone which journalist could join which unit. "I want you all to stop worrying," he finished. "We're going to make sure that after the war your boss comes up to you and gives you a slap on the back and compliments you on what a fine job you've done."

Hello, everybody! This was like the Ajax captain taking the referee aside before an important match against Feyenoord, putting his arm around him, and saying, "Don't you worry. We're going to make sure that the Football Association is very happy with you." The Israeli representatives had never been this shameless. The reaction from the folding chairs was more one of relief than howls of derision; I held my tongue, too, because I thought I might need that man one day—perhaps during a poison-gas attack.

The briefing had finished, and over the free snacks I bumped into a frustrated Dutch TV veteran. The U.S. army had little reason to place a journalist from an insignificant country like ours in an interesting army unit. The journalist had a choice: Sucking up and pleading to the army spokesman and then, after all that humiliation, still probably ending up in a field hospital in Kuwait or in an anti-aircraft defense facility in far-away Bahrain. Or he could lobby, for example via the Ministry of Defense in The Hague, who would only do something on the condition that you didn't embarrass them later. There you are in the desert, dependent on the soldiers around you for food and protection, and then they hear that on yesterday's news you talked about the serious human rights violation committed by three of those same soldiers.

The briefing at the Sheraton was my first glimpse of the polished steel of the American PR machine, and the television showed even more. The Israeli government had been good at manipulation, but now the creators of Disney World were at work. The best communications advisors, an army of spokespersons, unlimited resources . . . The mightiest ape in the jungle was stamping around here and not just in Kuwait. There were presentations at the UN with "proof" of the existence of Iraqi weapons-manufacturing plants, an unending stream of accusations of Iraqi involvement in September 11, and visionary speeches about democracy. Think tanks linked to the government plied editors with reports, opinion pieces, and other PR smart bombs. Central Command, the regional headquarters of the American army, sent an endless stream of communiqués into the world from a small podium in Qatar that it lavished $250,000 on to set up.

What a professional steamroller it was, and it resounded in the coverage—much louder and more clearly than in the Holy Land. The West was going to war, which meant enormous public interest, which meant that the Western media had to fill up their broadcasts and newspaper pages. But with what, if there were hardly any developments to report on? CNN provided the answer on a daily basis: The American army "media effort" delivered information each day; it was rarely news, but it was always "fit to print." Then they'd show another CNN frontman at CentCom: "It has now been confirmed that the third flight-deck mother ship has entered the Persian Gulf and will be ready for battle within the next seventy-two hours. The upper echelons can, of course, confirm nothing, but all indications are that an attack is imminent. Back to you, Jim."

The opponents also stuck to the Holy Land script. The

Iraqis were playing the Palestinians' role, and they managed to present an even weaker media policy. Every day, the Iraqi Minister of Information, Al-Sahhaf, appeared on all channels, uttering a medley of abuse and boasting ("My assessment is that, as usual . . . we will slaughter them all"). In his Arabic commentary, Al-Sahhaf used such strange expressions that I was not the only one who had to look up his abusive term for Americans and Brits—"*Uluzj*: An obscure term for untamed donkeys," it said in my dictionary.

The eccentric Al-Sahhaf was good for a short article; but, just like with the Palestinians, I wondered what would have happened if Saddam had seized upon the media attention to score a few points: "I'm being accused of secretly developing weapons of mass destruction, but why am I not allowed to do that when Israel can? Let's clear the whole region of weapons of mass destruction!"

With a decent PR office and a lobby of sympathizers, Saddam could have probably got such a suggestion onto the Western agenda. I could picture the bombardment of opinion pieces, letters, and columns, the introduction of government resolutions, and ready-made reports. Which Western government would have been able to speak out against a regional disarmament conference? But this was not the kind of campaign that Saddam fought; and as with the Palestinian Authority, his choice could be put down to the nature of dictatorship, as would be clear after the war. Saddam didn't want to clear the Middle East of weapons of mass destruction—as a dictator, you've got much more control at home if you can put down uprisings with a single blow, as the gassing of thousands of Kurds at the end of the 1980s had shown. The resistance had fallen apart after that. This was why Saddam had allowed the impression that he had those kinds of weapons to persist, right to the bitter end: It was to prevent an insurrection among his own subjects.

New faces, old patterns. Once again, nonviolent fundamentalist organizations were not allowed a voice. This allowed the American government to maintain that Saddam was working with Al-Qaida, and that the elimination of the Iraqi regime would be a blow to terrorism. This assertion would have probably been a little harder to sell if a larger proportion of the Western general public had known that Al-Qaida's main goal, on the contrary, was to overthrow secular Arab dictators like Saddam Hussein. The internal opposition in Iraq was actually made up of fundamentalists.

The parallels continued to mount up. I'd have liked to have had a look around Baghdad, but my visa application was repeatedly refused—a familiar frustration and not something you could explain to superiors and critics who'd never had any direct experience of dictatorship. How could Miss Germany visit Iraq, but the *NRC* newspaper not? I'd called, faxed, and offered bribes for weeks at a time . . . But somebody in the Iraqi Ministry of Information must have put a cross next to the *NRC*. All of the major Dutch media providers got into Iraq in the months before the invasion, apart from the *NRC*.

Old doubts began to resurface in my mind, such as whether the news media were really able to explain the nature of dictatorship. Did the hundreds of thousands of anti-war demonstrators in Europe know what Saddam did to his subjects? I was not aware that many of the demonstrators thought anything other than: "Of course dictators are bad, but war is really horrible, so we're against it under any circumstances— Peace, man!" I'd say dictatorship is war, too; a regime's war on its own people.

It was quite strange that many of the idealists who were now demonstrating against the invasion had been the ones calling for intervention during the Kosovo crisis, if necessary without UN permission: "We must do something." Saddam Hussein was a much more prolific murderer than Milosevic, and you wondered if the difference in media coverage played a part. During the Kosovo crisis, journalists could film the consequences of ethnic cleansing, and the brutality was given a face. This kind of striking reporting was not possible in Iraq; at best, you could get Iraqis who had fled the country years earlier to speak, if they dared to, because many had left relatives behind. But a talking head has much less impact— just ask the Palestinians who have to explain occupation.

In the run-up to the invasion there were blank spots, too. One of the largest was the reaction of ordinary Iraqis. The White House predicted that the American soldiers would be welcomed into the country as "liberators"—"with rice and flowers" was one of the expressions.

With the exception of a few donor darlings, almost all of the regimes and experts in the Arab world predicted a catastrophe for America. I didn't really find this very interesting, as my mistrust of Arab talking heads had grown too great. Of course the regimes were against an American invasion. It was being sold as a democratizing mission and, if it was a success, more would follow—hardly an alluring prospect for the dictators and kings in their Arab palaces.

There was one country where the reactions to the forthcoming invasion of Iraq did have some significance: Kuwait. The country had been occupied and devastated by Saddam Hussein in 1990, and America had chased him out six months later. Saddam had regularly threatened Kuwait with new attacks in the years following the liberation, which had catastrophic consequences for its economy and stock market. Who would invest in a country that might be plundered by Saddam at any moment?

If supporters for the invasion were to be found anywhere, it would be in Kuwait—most likely amongst the liberal members of the population. The war would bring democracy to Iraq; liberals want democracy; so you'd expect them to support the invasion.

I spoke to a ship owner, a businessman, a lawyer, an economist, and other liberal Kuwaitis. They were highly educated, spoke excellent English, and were charming, successful, and rich. They desperately wanted to be rid of Saddam, but they all asked a variation of the same question: Why should America bring democracy to Iraq if it was keeping dictators in the saddle in the rest of the region? Would a democratically chosen government in Baghdad really be able to beat an independent path, especially if it clashed with American interests? Would an Iraqi party be able to win an election with promises to support Palestine, to put up oil prices, to grant all contracts to Europe and China? Or was it the case that the White House wanted a "Saddam lite," who, just like all the other leaders of "moderate regimes," would renounce weapons of mass destruction, pass commissions on to the American business community and, at worst, be slightly antagonistic towards Israel.

If I'd been at the beginning of my posting, I would have felt compelled to try to get this into the news. The Americans thought they'd be met with joy and open arms, but even the most pro-American Arabs in the region, the Kuwaiti liberals—the ones who wanted a society built on an American model and who owed their freedom to the American liberation of their country—didn't trust them.

By now I knew, as I conducted the interviews, that these liberals would not get much further than the background features in the media, or not even that far. One by one, they'd say somewhere during the conversation, "This is off the record, you know, no names . . ." with a winning smile, to mask the humiliation of a successful economist well into his fifties not daring to share his opinions with a guy in his early thirties. If there's no first name or surname available, news is instantly rendered a little less "fit to print"; but the lack of a journalistic hook has an even greater effect. Kuwait was not a democracy: There were no free parliamentary votes, no demonstrations, strikes, or other news events to which correspondents could hitch the liberals' objections. Try imagining this report: "Today in Kuwait, thousands of people marched against Western support of their dictators. They demanded the dismantlement of the secret Western bank accounts in which dictators hoard their loot, and chanted slogans against the generous commissions that Western defense companies pay out to dictators and their entourages. Banners displayed protests against Western training and armament of the Arab secret services who torture and murder on a large scale."

Instead, the liberal Kuwaits sunk into the "background," where other problems played out. In order to explain the mistrust of the pro-Western Arabs, you'd have to recount that, despite the American story about democracy being brought to the region, in fact all kinds of dictators were being supported. But how did you get such Western support onto television? CIA agents don't allow any cameras to be present when they explain to their Arab associates the latest insights that have been attained about how to break somebody both psychologically and physically. The American businessman with a CIA past will not let a journalist record how he sold the latest eavesdropping technology to a befriended Arabic secret service at far above the market price, with the profits being shared between them. There are no images of Western secret agents flying terror suspects to Arab countries so they can torture them out of reach of human rights stipulations. Remember: No images, no story.

I'd spoken to another fellow journalist during the briefing given by the American army at the Sheraton hotel. "Have you just got here?" he'd asked me. "You'd better hurry up. The farmers in the North are the story. They can work their fields for the last time tomorrow, because after that the American army will be there. I've got names and numbers."

I nodded thankfully and, despite my five years' experience, I was still astonished that something so inane could be the story. But the explanation was simple: The Anglo-American media machine was dominating the news stream and, within that, the story was the build-up of American troops. When were they going to strike? The evacuation of the farmers was a good illustration of this—one that you could easily get a shot of in the constant competition for space amongst newspaper journalists.

It had all been shown before. A sophisticated media campaign lays down an image—rice and flowers—and it becomes hard to shift afterwards. Just think how impossible an honest Q&A session would sound:

Our correspondent is in Kuwait. Do the Kuwaitis think that America will succeed in bringing democracy?

Many Kuwaitis do not believe this to be America's plan.

But there are pro-American Kuwaitis, aren't there?
They are against it as well, because they don't trust America.

What percentage of the population thinks this way?
Umm . . . I'm not sure. It might be just the people I've spoken to. It is a dictatorship, you see.

That was our correspondent. We're going directly to Washington for a long-awaited speech by President Bush on America's historic mission to spread freedom. But, before that, a report on the farmers in northern Kuwait who worked their land for the last time yesterday as a consequence of the build-up of American troops.

That was why the army spokesmen in the Sheraton was so relaxed. He had us all chained up, and he knew it.

Chapter 14

"There's Money in the Flag"

I was going to quit my job after the fall of Baghdad, so once the American troops entered Iraq I knew that my final weeks on the ground had arrived. It would be a revealing time, but in the beginning I saw only the repetition of familiar patterns. Was the fighting being done by "Zionist crusaders," "American and British invading troops?" or by "allies?" Were their opponents the "Iraqi national resistance" or "Saddam loyalists?" Were we seeing a "heavy bombardment of densely populated cities" or "Operation Shock and Awe," a name that Sony claimed for a new computer game while the war was still being fought.

Each camp had its own terminology, and played the good guy in its own version of events. Fox News reported accusations of Iraqi cooperation with Al-Qaida as fact, and reasoned

221

accordingly: How, then, could Europeans be against the elimination of the man behind September 11? Of course, they hate America! Hezbollah TV did the same with the accusation that Israel's Mossad had committed the attack: How, then, could Americans blame Iraq? Of course, they hate Islam!

I followed the war from the capital city of an important Arab country—the place where I'd started out five years earlier, *Umm iddunya*, the mother of the world, Cairo. Behind the scenes, the Egyptian government was helping the Americans where it could, but what was going on among the population? This was a blank spot, but because of the war there was now so much extra space in the newspaper that we could show the contours of those blank spots. I began a newspaper column, "The Arab Street." I walked through the city and struck up conversations with ordinary Egyptians, doing the previously mentioned vox pops. On television, these could never be more than quick flashes: "It's against Islam . . . very bad"—if the people dared speak at all. An article offered more room, and you could present the speakers anonymously:

> Of course it is God's punishment. Allah is almighty, so everything that happens is His will. The recent earthquake in Turkey cannot be separated from the manner in which Turkey has renounced Islam; and I hardly have to explain AIDS, do I? The Imam said it, too, just now. The American invasion is punishment for our lack of piety. Everybody is concerned with money and a house, a mobile telephone . . . We have just prayed for a fast end to it, that the Americans lose quickly and leave. Egypt has big responsibilities, because it is the cradle of civilization.[14]

If the Americans were real Christians they wouldn't do this. Why are they interfering? Each people has its own system and its own leader. We love Mubarak, and Mubarak loves us. During the First Gulf War I worked in Iraq as a patissier. After the bombardments, Saddam would come out onto the street. People could touch him, and it was obvious that everybody loved him and that he loved the people.[15]

America is the strongest country in the world because it consists of fifty states, but the second-strongest army in the world is Iraq's and they are up against that now. This is why Germany is against the war; they realize that they will be next. Bush has said that God made him president in order to deliver the world from Islam. That Bush . . . I read recently that Israeli soldiers laid bets on pregnant Palestinian women—will it be a boy or a girl? Then they'd cut the woman open to see who was right. They also undress women and drive them around Israel in metal cages. I get so angry when I hear things like that. How could you do such a thing?[16]

Politics is for politicians. I'm just an ordinary civil servant, and in the evening I drive a taxi. The war? To be honest, I don't follow it that much. I get home at midnight and I have to be up at six. At that point I don't feel like poring over the news. It's terrible, people say. An attack on Islam. I hope it's over quickly.[17]

Did you know that Israel is going to blow up the Al-Aqsa mosque once Baghdad falls? That was the headline of my *Al-Usbu* newspaper yesterday. Nearly all of Clinton's and

Bush's advisors are Jewish. Some of them openly, others in secret. Secret Jews, like Saddam. He invaded Kuwait so that Americans could put down troops in the Gulf, close to the oil and the holy sites. They weaken Islam because Jews know that they can't do much against a strong Islam.[18]

I wrote it all down, and the *NRC*'s inbox filled up: Your correspondent is making Arabs look ridiculous. It proved again that you have to have had this kind of conversation yourself—then you know that people say this kind of thing without hesitation and more in a tone of resignation than anger. They only get angry when you start contradicting them.

It was a strange routine. During the daytime I had the conversations for "The Arab Street," and in the evenings I watched television. It resembled the beginning of my correspondent's job when Iraq was being bombed during Operation Desert Fox and I was summarizing press releases from my hotel room in Amman. I didn't have to do that anymore, because I'd stopped doing radio and television, and the *NRC* only asked for background.

So I had time to watch television, and gradually something occurred to me—not what was said and shown on the Western channels, but precisely what was not said and shown. In the run-up to the invasion, the authoritative Anglosphere media had adopted the perspective of the American PR machine, and this continued during the war. The embedded journalists who'd been assigned to the front by the army spokesman in the Kuwait Sheraton provided images of soldiers ducking away from enemy fire, crawling under walls, and reaching a position from where they could eliminate the enemy. The Iraqi enemy remained faceless, whereas you did get to see the fear, tension, or relief on the faces of the Americans. It was like a video game—game over for the newly beaten division of the Republican Guard, and America through to the next level, with a new army division.

It was the good guy/bad guy Hollywood approach, and nearly all the analyzes coincided with the one that Central Command had sent from Qatar: The conquest of the port city Umm Qasr had top priority—not for military reasons, but to "get humanitarian goods to the Iraqi people as quickly as possible." Fighting inside the city should be prevented, not because America's technological advantage would be largely lost and many of their own would perish, but because "street fighting would result in many civilian casualties." At the end of the day, it was about the hearts and minds of the Iraqi people; reporters and army spokesmen chimed this tune in chorus, implying that the war was a good thing, and that we just needed to explain this to the people of Iraq.

Every last crumb that was dropped from the Central Command podium was hoovered up. CNN called it "Be the first to know"—news as a competition. "We've just had confirmation from CentCom that Umm Qasr is now in the hands of American commandos. Back to you, Jim." In the 1991 Gulf War, the same thing happened, only at that time there weren't any Arabic broadcasters with their own correspondents refuting American statements. Now you could zap from Jim to Al-Jazeera, where they were in the middle of a live telephone conversation with the Iraqi commander in Umm Qasr.

"We now have confirmation." Did the CNN and BBC journalists believe that themselves? Surely they were aware that the army's task was not to deliver reliable information, but to neutralize the enemy with minimal losses? And if you have to lie to achieve this . . . All's fair in love and war.

Beside all those American press conferences, wouldn't it have been an idea to remind people how the media had been deceived twelve years earlier? Iraq had trampled Kuwait underfoot, and the White House was intent on a military expedition; but, according to opinion polls, the majority of the American populace were against it—until a fifteen-year-old Kuwaiti girl testified in front of the Congress that she'd seen Iraqi soldiers taking babies from their incubators and letting them die on the floor, so that the incubators could go directly to Baghdad. The witness statement was shown on television, and support for the liberation of Kuwait shot up. Long after, it came out that this "nurse" was the daughter of the Kuwaiti ambassador in Washington, and that she'd been pushed forward by the communications consultancy Hill & Knowlton. Just like it only became known years later that the American flags with which the Kuwaitis "spontaneously" welcomed their liberators had been provided by the communications consultancy The Rendon Group.

Why, in the middle of this flood of PR from CentCom, was the Western media not open about the way it had been manipulated in the past? For a while, I considered the fly-on-the-wall theory—the tendency that journalists have to believe that they are just observing without being influenced. But that was not the only thing that was off-screen on Western channels.

Western correspondents and presenters often referred to Iraq's instability; after all, the country is made up of three population groups with little in common—Kurds in the north, Sunnis in the center, and Shiites in the south. There was rarely any explanation after those five sentences as to how that had come about. Until the end of World War I, the areas had been independent provinces of a Turkish colonial empire; then they were captured by Great Britain and added to Iraq. It was like grouping Poles, northern Germans, and northern Dutch people together, and telling them they were now a new country. It was a recipe for instability, which was Britain's intention: An unstable Iraq would remain dependent on British aid and protection, and would do what London wanted. As the former American foreign minister Henry Kissinger put it in his classic work *Diplomacy*: "The borders of the Middle East had been drawn by foreign, largely European, powers at the end of the First World War in order to facilitate their domination of the area." That was why so many borders in the Arab world were straight lines— Western governments had drawn them using a ruler on a map, and they certainly didn't have the local populations' interests at heart.

"Anti-Western feelings" in the Middle East received a lot of airplay in reports in the Western media. You might think that a couple of minutes of historical explanation would have been in order to understand this—for example, about Iran. Iran had a democratic government in the 1950s but, when prime minister Mossadeq decided to nationalize the oil industry, the CIA put the Shah on the throne in a coup d"etat. The shah rebuilt the country into a pro-Western dictatorship with a ubiquitous and merciless secret service and awe-inspiring corruption—a mirror of some current Arab regimes. The anger around this discharged itself in the "anti-Western Islamic Revolution." To put down the Islamic Revolution, Western governments armed Saddam with poison gas, amongst other things, during the Iran–Iraq war. But they also secretly gave weapons to Iran, in exchange for which

Iran released Western hostages in Lebanon—the Iran Contra scandal. Henry Kissinger again: "Too bad they both can't lose." A million people died.

And then came Osama Bin Laden. How many Western viewers knew that, for years, people like him had been trained and armed by the CIA? This could be explained in a few words, too: In 1979, the Soviet Union had invaded Afghanistan to help the collapsing communist regime. In response, the CIA, together with Saudi Arabia and Pakistan, set up the *mujahideen* (the jihad warriors). They fought a guerrilla war against the Russians, which the *mujahideen*—amongst whose members was Osama Bin Laden—won, after which some went to fight against the Egyptian regime, while others got involved in the Algerian civil war. When Saddam invaded Kuwait, Bin Laden offered to chase him out with his warriors, but the Gulf States preferred to call in America's assistance. Bin Laden saw this as definitive proof that the regimes were only out for self-preservation, even if it meant calling in the Western powers that had caused the problems in the Islamic world in the first place. Bin Laden shifted his goals, which led to the 9/11 attacks, which formed the justification for the invasion of Iraq . . . and the circle was complete.

You might think that this kind of background material would be part of the equation for Western viewers. There was air time enough, and if thousands of dollars a day could be spent on sending a reporter in Baghdad to summarize the reports from the news agencies, there had to be a budget for documentaries or other short features which explained the role that Western governments had played in the Middle East in recent decades. Why was this so rarely mentioned on Western stations as the bombs rained down on Baghdad?

There was more than this left untold on mainstream Western news bulletins. While Arabic stations showed the human consequences of the bombardment every hour, the Western ones did something else. Every evening, the graphics departments conjured up a sort of Risk board of the region, complete with maps, aircraft, boats, tanks, little figures, arrows, and yellow and red stars. In the repeated clips or CNN promos, you'd see fighter jets landing on aircraft carriers, the pilot giving the thumbs up: Yep, got rid of the bombs. Computer animations showed how the stealth bomber could dodge the radar. Look how clever we are, the films said. We can make a rocket that can seek out a toilet seat after a six-hundred-kilometers flight, left down the stairs, and boom.

There were no computer animations showing what happened after the boom—how a cluster bomb threw out 140 mines, each strong enough to destroy a tank. A few never go off, and so you get unexploded mines left around in places where children play. Nor was there any computer mapping of what happens to a human body when a new-generation bomb vacuum-implodes the surroundings.

Your correspondent sat in a hotel room shaking his fist at the television. After a couple of evenings like this, he wrote the following piece:

> I experienced a bombardment myself, and I think of it often these days. It was in Gaza, and in terms of range and duration it was nothing compared to what the people of Baghdad, Mosul, and Tikrit have suffered over the past six days. However, there are some parallels. You always hear about civilian casualties and wounded, and if the

body count doesn't get too high, it's a "clean" war. What nonsense.

If you are somewhere where bombs are being dropped, what you feel more than anything is powerlessness. Your life is in the hands of someone behind a control panel or in a cockpit. He can make a decision that will leave you dead or handicapped. In Gaza, I felt such nauseating fear that I immediately had to plaster another emotion on top. The Palestinians around me seemed to be doing that, too, and together we put on a stage show. Oh, there goes another bomb, ho ho. We'd have been capable of dancing for the cameras like you see Iraqis doing on their national television right now. "Defiant Iraqis after last night's bombing," CNN sometimes subtitles such images. "Iraqis unbroken after last night's bombing."

It's rubbish. Palestinian aid workers in Gaza talked about an explosive increase in domestic violence, spontaneous miscarriages, and heart attacks. Babies' first words were not baba or mama, but "bomb," "martyr," and "airplane." Drawings of fighter jets, bullets, and blood, from children who want to join the army when they grow up instead of becoming footballers or actors, and who don't play tag but instead play soldiers and undertakers. In the words of a local psychologist, "They shout *Allahu akbar* for the cameras, but at night they wet their beds." Parents no longer dare to make love because they're afraid an attack will begin and they'll have to run quickly to their children. One Gaza father recounted how his eight-year-old would secretly get dressed again before going to sleep so she could run straight to the shelter during a bombing.

The hysterical phone calls once the network is back up—did everyone make it? Is the family business still standing? Has it been plundered? Insurance policies don't pay out for war damage, and most people don't even have insurance. When the bombs are falling you can't go outside. This also includes ambulances and fire engines, so if you fall down the stairs or have some other kind of accident you have to wait for the all-clear. This makes parents even more nervous, because when bombs are going off children run all over the place. They hide in the bathroom or try to sprint down the street. Naturally they ask when it's going to stop.

Aid workers told me that Palestinian parents are so desperate to reassure their children that they say, tomorrow. Or, in an hour. But the bombing continues, and the children lose their trust in their parents, their last place of refuge.

This is what I miss most in the media: Images of small children crawling into a hole, hysterically hitting and kicking their parents because they are so confused; stories of adolescent girls who mutilate themselves because this is a kind of pain they are in control of themselves; that during the bombing, verses from the Koran are played through the mosque's loud speakers to help people through their mortal terror. I never see this, and not on Al-Jazeera either. They stick to the Arab taboo against showing vulnerability and sorrow, and accompany their gruesome images of the dead and wounded with texts about the "heroic perseverance of the Iraqi people." The Gaza bombardment taught me this at least—the term "clean war" belongs with notions like pregnant virgins and democratic dictators.[19]

I heard later that this happens quite often to correspondents: A turbulent period brings up memories of other similarly intense periods, and you suddenly need to give way to the feelings you'd repressed at the time. There was no other article in my career that got so many reactions— an illustration that you can often only place your best work outside the stock journalistic genres.

That would be the sort of material that could bring out the reality of war. Have a veteran sniper describe what it's like to pick out Iraqis as if they were ducks: American weapons have such a long range that the Iraqis would never realize that anyone was around, until the bullet hit. Or let an Israeli explain street fighting. You're walking down an alleyway, and suddenly a door opens. You shoot before looking, because if you do it the other way round, and it's a guy with a gun, you're a goner. Only it's a surprised-looking eight-year-old girl in her nightdress who crumples to the floor.

That's war, but the reporting on CNN more often resembled the advertisements that armies use to recruit soldiers: "The marines enlarge your world." "Above all—the air force." Arabic stations did show unimaginably atrocious images of distraught grandmothers and blown-up children's heads, hour after hour, though in a way that was more likely to arouse anger and defiance in the viewer than sadness and compassion. Another image I couldn't get out of my head was of some Iraqi soldiers shot dead in a foxhole, the white flag still grasped in their hands.

At such moments, the gulf between East and West seemed to widen, not because we are different from each other, but because we are shown radically different images of the world. Day after day, Arabs watched distraught Iraqis whose families had just been blown to bits, limbs all over the place, everything lost. And then they heard the American president triumphantly bragging about the victory with one eye on the next election, and dismissing a question about "collateral damage" as incidental casualties.

If the Western mass media had done their job during the war, viewers would have sat in front of their television sets crying and vomiting. Did this not happen because hardly anyone with war experience ever works on the editorial teams? Was it because some editors found the military toys with cool names like Apache, Tomahawk, and Daisy Cutter exciting? I worry it was something much worse. Before the war was over, the *International Herald Tribune* revealed the advice that the major American broadcasters had received from their communications consultancies. These marketing experts help the stations find out what their public like to watch. American broadcasters are commercial outfits, after all. The recommendations were clear: The more nationalistic the reporting, the higher the viewing figures would be. There should be no anti-war demonstrations, no pitiful stories about the victims, and a lot of anthem-playing, fatherland imagery, and fluttering stars and stripes—in the studio, in the logo, in the filler clips. One consultant summed it up in five words: "There's money in the flag." And so it turned out. Forty of the fifty most watched programs in America during the war were from Fox News, who described Saddam Hussein as "the big, bad boy from Baghdad," who adopted the full terminology, approach, and subject matter fed to them by CentCom in Qatar, and who described the anti-war protests in Europe as "organized by communists."

That was one more essential filter in the news: The customers. In Europe, too, the ratings showed that people would rather be told things by their familiar anchorman than by a boring-looking expert. They'd rather watch short films on Us against Them than complex analyzes on conflicting interests, let alone historical background pieces that made their own country look bad. In Europe, as in America, the editors-in-chief were primarily judged on their circulation and viewing figures.

It made you sadder, if not wiser, and the months and years that followed the invasion gave no reason for optimism. American soldiers in Iraq were not welcomed with rice and flowers, but with bombs and grenades. Although there was never proof of an Iraqi collaboration with Al-Qaida, five years after 9/11 almost the half of the American public still believed that Saddam Hussein had been responsible for the attacks and that most of the hijackers had been Iraqis. The idea that the Iraqis would welcome American troops turned out to have been introduced by the Iraqi opposition in exile, who had used the communications consultancy The Rendon Group—the same company that had provided the flags after the American liberation of Kuwait. And the scene on Paradise Square where Iraqis had toppled the giant statue of Saddam Hussein to loud jubilation—"Baghdad celebrates liberation?" It turned out not to have been a massive national festival after all, but something put together by perhaps two hundred Iraqis and a sharp American army officer. Back to you, Jim.

Afterword

Events in this book cover the period between 1998 and 2003, and some things have changed a lot since then. The Muslim Brotherhood now blogs. A number of Arab-language TV news stations have begun operating. Footage of Egyptian police brutality appears on YouTube. Young people use their telephones to secretly film sexual harrassment on the street and put it on Facebook. Ariel Sharon and Yasser Arafat have left the stage, a new American administration is in, wars were fought in Gaza and South Lebanon. In Egypt an apparently truly independent newspaper, *Almasri Alyowm* (*The Egyptian Today*) seems set to wipe out the state-run competition, fundamentally altering at least the print media landscape in that country.

At the same time, a lot has remained essentially the same since 2003. Mainstream news coverage of the Middle East is still structured the way it was a few years ago, and there still has been no fundamental debate about the pros and cons of Western support for Arab dictators, and how such decades-long support is to be reconciled with the professed ideals of "freedom-loving" Western governments. Little effort has been made to explain the motives, dilemmas, and self-image of groups such as Al-Qaida, making it harder to defeat them. And the NATO and Israeli PR machines still go largely uncovered, and continue to have the upper hand in imposing their vocabulary and frames of reference. I am not aware of a single mainstream medium anywhere in the world that explains its choice of topics, angles, terminology, and its criteria for hearing some parties to a conflict, but not others.

When this book appeared in the Netherlands in the summer of 2006, I decided not to include an afterword with suggestions for change. It seemed to me that the problems are so big and diverse that they require a fundamental rethink of the news industry's basic assumptions. Since there were no obvious instant solutions, I hoped there would be a debate about the problems themselves.

This was a mistake, as I should have known from the book itself. If you don't frame a message yourself, others will do that for you—and you may not recognize what you see. In this case, the book was said by reviewers, colleagues, and columnists to claim that "journalism is useless." Some of my Dutch colleagues even put together a whole book in order to refute this claim and demonstrate how useful they are. It was delightfully absurd: You write a book with the message that every message gets distorted when covered in the media, and what happens? This message gets distorted, too.

Perhaps colleagues were not stupid, but jealous, because in the Netherlands alone this book has now sold an incomprehensible quarter of a million copies. It is also out now in Hungary, Italy, Denmark, and Germany, and in some of these countries I've had funny encounters and confrontations with colleagues, too. They would say, okay, tell me in one sentence what your book's about, and I would answer: The book is about the impossibility of saying in one sentence what a situation is about. Colleagues would laugh more or less obligingly, and then press again: Look, we only have twelve seconds for this quote.

In retrospect, I wish I had had at my disposal at the time the one-sentence framework which I came up with only recently: This book is about factors that lie beyond the control of journalists, but that influence what those journalists cover, and how. The way forward, then, would be to no longer ignore, hide, or obscure those factors, but somehow to integrate them in one's coverage, thereby helping unsuspecting viewers and readers to better understand what they see and read.

How? There seem at least five main problems with coverage as it is right now. First, the news media need to find ways to alert their audiences that this is what they are following: The news. Until 9/11 no one in the West, except for Western Muslims and a small circle of professional experts, knew much about Islam. Then Al-Qaida made Islam news—as we know, news is about problems and conflicts—and, as a result, Western audiences have been fed hundreds and hundreds of stories that put Islam and violence together in one frame. Small wonder, then, that many have come to the conclusion that Islam is inherently violent. It is not the journalists' fault that they highlight mostly problems and conflicts, because these are what news is usually about. But it is the responsibility of journalists to make sure that their audiences realize that what they see is the exception, and not the rule.

The same goes for so-called "background" information. The problem these days with the media is not that it is impossible to find good background stuff; witness publications such as the *Economist*, the BBC, and NPR documentaries, and longer pieces in the *New York Review of Books* and the *London Review of Books*. The problem is that hardly anyone reads these things, and that without this so-called background stuff, news in the foreground is incomprehensible. As a German reviewer pointed out, there is among journalists this cop-out mechanism that as long as readers and viewers can find the good stuff somewhere in the media landscape, it doesn't really matter that the rest of it is full of below-par material.

A second avenue for change concerns coverage of nondemocratic societies. A place like Syria is not a country with an army; it is an army with a country. This is obscured from view by the regime's use of labels that are familiar to us: President, parliament, police, party . . . But an altogether different system hides behind this facade. That is why journalism in a police state is impossible or, rather, a contradiction in terms; a dictatorship in which journalism as we know it is possible would cease to be a dictatorship.

Some colleagues and reviewers have countered that this is a matter of effort: You simply need to work harder and have better contacts. But if you do this, and manage to find an opposition member prepared to be quoted, and verify some facts, such "success" would be the biggest failure of all. By producing a news article that was in no way different from a news item about a democratic country, you would have inadvertently hidden the most important thing of all: That the country you are covering is not a democracy at all, and everything that this entails.

Once you accept that the classical fit-to-print methods of journalism are suited only to the sort of political system they grew out of—democracies—a space opens up for non-conventional reporting. What that space might look like, I wish I knew.

Third, we need to incorporate in coverage the fact that while news represents the world, this representation then influences that same world. In particular, something needs to be done about the impunity with which PR firms and communications departments operate. They can do so because mainstream media continue to pretend they are not really there. If a reporter goes into a battle zone embedded with the army, this should not merely be pointed out—it should take center stage. The reporter should preface pretty much everything that he or she says with a sentence that goes something like: "Of course, I have no idea what they are keeping from me and I cannot talk to the other side, but what strikes me so far on this tour with the marines is . . ." Naturally, this requires the sort of fundamental rethink of basic assumptions mentioned earlier. Much of the glamour and posturing that war correspondents revel in suddenly become pretty ridiculous when you enlarge the frame and reveal how they really operate.

This point ties in with another area for improvement: The news media are a countervailing power to politicians and corporations, and when media fail this can have serious consequences. Hence, when the media are caught exaggerating or lying (either by omission or commission), they should be treated by other media in the same way that cheating politicians and corporations are treated. When CNN tells a lie, the impact may be much bigger than when my silly little Dutch government does. Yet in the latter case it is considered news; in the former case, it ends up somewhere on the "media page," at best.

Two more suggestions. News media need to level with their audiences about the variousness of possible perspectives about a given subject. Readers and viewers need to be reminded that the only consensus is that there is no consensus. Even about this.

Websites seem ideally suited to deliver those perspectives. Have a foreign editor use "separation barrier," or "Apartheid wall" or "fence" or whatever other term is available for that concrete thing on the West Bank. I mean in Judea and Samaria. In the Palestinian territories. In the occupied—oh no, disputed—territories. Or is it "liberated?"

As I have tried to demonstrate in this book, the issue goes further than vocabulary. It would be marvelous to read more than one interpretation of a news event, especially when that interpretation is tied to an explanation of the underlying worldview. Al-Qaida frames most of its actions in defensive terms. If we want to understand Al-Qaida's appeal, we need to see how it presents itself—not only how the Western foreign-policy establishment views it.

Who knows what a wonderful narrative technique such explanations may prove to be. Foreign desks have a great deal of expertise and experience that help them decide why a story is news, or not, what the angle should be, etc. Why not experiment with a column, either in the paper or on the web, in which the foreign editor writes a daily update about the criteria behind that day's journalistic choices? It could take you through the day's news, pointing out the grey areas of doubt, the blank areas on the map, the stories they would have liked to do but were prevented from running by factors beyond their control . . .

Finally, there are the simplifications and nationalisms inherent in all market-based news media. Here, I am even more clueless. Somehow in the history of our democracies, it has been decided that news should be treated as a product rather than as a good. A product belongs on the market, where the most popular version prevails. A good belongs in civil society, together with, for example, the protection afforded by the police and the justice afforded by the justice system. (In Europe, health care is also seen as a good.)

It is very difficult to see how democracies can survive when the information on which voters base their ballot-box decisions reflects not what they need to hear, but what they like to hear. If you give people only the food they say they want, they become obese. If you give them only the information they want, they become ignorant and self-righteous. Yes, the United States elected Barack Obama, but its underlying information infrastructure is as defunct as ever. Unless this changes, sooner or later another ignorant, gung-ho populist will win the elections, plunging the U.S.—and the democratic West with it—into another disastrous military adventure.

A final paradox: The sort of people for whom I wrote this book and afterword are the least likely to read it. But maybe I'm just a pessimist from old Europe. I hope so.

PS: For reasons that should be clear by now, I have changed many names. As well, some of the articles I have quoted have been edited for brevity.

Notes

1 *De Volkskrant*, 21 November 1998
2 *De Volkskrant*, 7 August 1998
3 *De Volkskrant*, 14 August 1998
4 *De Volkskrant*, 7 December 1998
5 *De Volkskrant*, 8 October 1998
6 *De Volkskrant*, 6 October 1998
7 *De Volkskrant*, 8 February 1999
8 *Al-Gumhuriya*, 28 September 1999
9 NRC Handelsblad, 27 December 2001
10 NRC Handelsblad, 15 March 2001
11 NRC Handelsblad, 3 August 2002
12 NRC Handelsblad, 2 February 2002
13 NRC Handelsblad, 3 April 2002
14 NRC Handelsblad, 28 March 2003
15 NRC Handelsblad, 28 March 2003
16 NRC Handelsblad, 20 March 2003
17 NRC Handelsblad, 24 March 2003

18 NRC Handelsblad, 25 March 2003
19 NRC Handelsblad, 25 March 2003